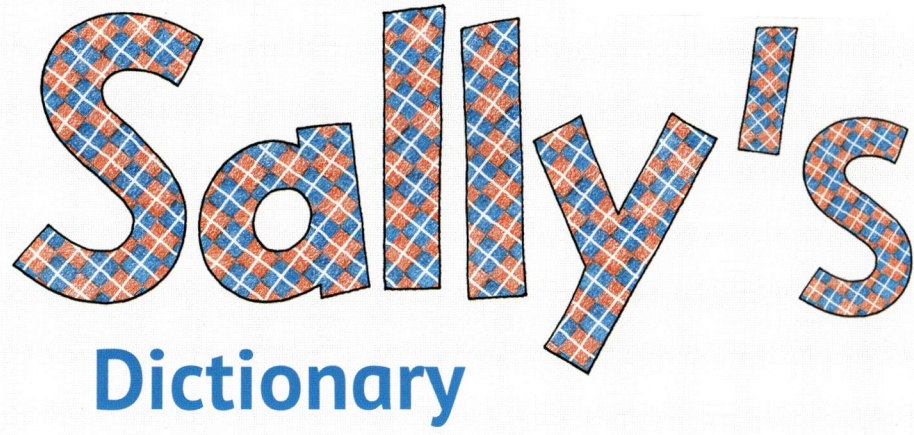

Sally's

Dictionary

Wörterbuch für die Grundschule

Erarbeitet von

Jasmin Brune
Daniela Elsner
Stefanie Gleixner-Weyrauch
Marion Lugauer
Sabine Schwarz

Illustriert von

Barbara Jung

Oldenbourg Schulbuchverlag, München

Audioquellen

S. 10: The happy kangaroo song, reproduced by permission of Oxford Universitiy Press, from: Carolin Graham,
Children Jazz Chants Old & New, © Oxford University Press, 2002
S. 30: The clothes song, T: Stefanie Gleixner Weyrauch/M: Thomas Blendinger
S. 46: Ice cream rock, T: Stefanie Gleixner Weyrauch/M: Thomas Blendinger
S. 50: I'm a little teapot, T:/M: George Harry Sanders, Clarence Kelley © Marilyn Sanders Music

Lizenz BOOKii

Tessloff Verlag, Ragnar Tessloff GmbH & Co. KG, Nürnberg, **www.tessloff.com**
BOOKii® ist eine eingetragene Marke des Tessloff Verlags, Nürnberg

Redaktion: Bea Herrmann
Illustration: Barbara Jung
Kapitelvignetten: Wilfried Poll
Umschlagkonzept: Mendell & Oberer, München
Umschlagillustration: Barbara Jung
Technische Umsetzung: fidus Publikations-Service GmbH, Nördlingen

www.cornelsen.de

1. Auflage, 5. Druck 2025

Alle Drucke dieser Auflage sind inhaltlich unverändert
und können im Unterricht nebeneinander verwendet werden.

© 2017 Cornelsen Verlag GmbH, Mecklenburgische Str. 53, 14197 Berlin, E-Mail: service@cornelsen.de

Druck: H. Heenemann, Berlin

ISBN 978-3-637-20402-7

PEFC-zertifiziert
Dieses Produkt
stammt aus
nachhaltig
bewirtschafteten
Wäldern

PEFC
PEFC/04-31-1156   **www.pefc.de**

Inhalt

Benutzerhinweise 4

Hello 10

Colours and numbers .. 14

At school 18

Body and feelings 22

Toys 26

Clothes 30

Weather and days 34

Around the year 38

Family and friends 42

Vegetables and fruit ... 46

Breakfast 50

Pets and farm animals 54

Transport 58

Halloween 62

Christmas 66

At home 70

Lunch 74

Hobbies and sports 78

My day 82

Shopping 86

Wild animals 90

At the doctor's 94

Jobs 98

Meeting people 102

Anhang

Verbs 108

Adjectives 110

Prepositions 112

Numbers 114

Time 115

Grammar 116

Useful phrases 118

Words: Englisch – Deutsch 120

Wörter: Deutsch – Englisch 136

Hello, my name is Sally.

Das ist das Känguru Sally. Sally begleitet dich durch das Wörterbuch und hat sich im Wimmelbild jedes Kapitels versteckt.
Mach dich auf die Suche, indem du immer zuerst den Auftrag „Find Sally." antippst.
Wenn du Sally dann gefunden hast, tippst du sie mit dem Hörstift an.

Die Wörter im Wimmelbild kannst du selbst erlesen oder dir vom Hörstift vorlesen lassen. Unter dem Wimmelbild kannst du verschiedene Aufgaben lösen. Gleich nach der Wimmelbildseite findest du passende Wörter und Sätze zum Nachschlagen.
Hier sind alle Nomen blau, alle Verben rot und alle Adjektive grün. In den Cartoons kannst du nachlesen, wie man diese Wörter in Gesprächen verwendet.

Nach dem letzten Kapitel findest du einen Anhang mit wichtigen Wörtern und Sätzen, Erklärungen und Regeln.
Am Ende des Wörterbuches gibt es eine alphabetische Wörterliste mit den Wörtern aus allen Kapiteln auf Deutsch und auf Englisch.
Achtung: Die Seiten im Anhang sind nicht vertont.

So verwendest du den Hörstift:

Schalte den Hörstift ein.
Aktiviere den Hörstift für das Wörterbuch, indem du damit auf das Symbol auf der vorderen Umschlagseite innen tippst.
Dann verbindest du den Hörstift über ein Kabel mit einem internetfähigen Computer.
So lädst du den Akku auf und gleichzeitig alle Dateien, die zum Wörterbuch gehören, herunter.

Los geht's: Schlage eine Wimmelseite oder eine Seite mit Wörterliste auf.
Alle englischen Wörter und Sprechblasen auf diesen Seiten kannst du dir vorlesen lassen, indem du sie mit dem Hörstift antippst.
Manchmal stehen Wörter nicht auf weißem Untergrund, sondern sind direkt in das Bild hineingezeichnet. Wenn du dieses Symbol))) daran findest, wird dir die Schrift im Bild vorgelesen, wenn du das Symbol antippst.
Dieses Symbol ♫ zeigt dir jeweils an, dass du dir hier ein Lied oder einen Reim anhören kannst.

Wenn du dich mit einer Wimmelseite beschäftigst, ist es sinnvoll, sich erst einmal alle Wörter und Sprechblasen im Bild vorlesen zu lassen.
Dann kannst du die Suchaufträge lösen, die mit diesem Symbol ? gekennzeichnet sind. Um sie mit deinem Hörstift lösen zu können, musst du sie zunächst antippen und dir vorlesen lassen.

Auf den Seiten 6/7 und 8/9 werden dir alle Funktionen der Seiten mit Wimmelbildern oder Wörterlisten noch einmal an Beispielen erklärt.

Dabei hilft dir das Wörterbuch:

1. Du möchtest wissen, wie ein deutsches Wort auf Englisch heißt oder wie ein englisches Wort geschrieben wird. Ab S. 136 findest du eine deutsche Wörterliste, die nach dem ABC geordnet ist. Suche das deutsche Wort. Du findest das englische Wort daneben.
2. Wenn du wissen möchtest, wie ein englisches Wort auf Deutsch heißt, findest du ab S. 120 eine englische Wörterliste, die nach dem ABC geordnet ist.
3. Du suchst mehr Wörter zu einem Thema. Suche im Inhaltsverzeichnis das passende Thema. Schlage die entsprechenden Seiten auf und lies nach.
4. Du suchst Verben, Adjektive, Präpositionen oder Zahlen bzw. Uhrzeiten? Schlage ab S. 106 nach.
5. Du möchtest eine Regel nachlesen? Schau auf S. 114/115 nach.

So wirst du ein Wörterbuch-Profi:

Suche folgende Kapitel: *Hello, Toys, Breakfast, Hobbies and sports, Christmas.*
Schreibe so: Hello: Page 10 – 13

Was heißen folgende Wörter auf Englisch?
Fuß, fliegen, glücklich, kalt, Tante, verstecken
Suche in der Wörterliste ab S. 136. Schreibe so: Fuß – foot
Was heißen folgende Wörter auf Deutsch?
elephant, funny, to put on, sky, to wash, wet
Suche in der Wörterliste ab S. 120. Schreibe so: elephant – Elefant

Suche im Kapitel *Weather and days* drei Adjektive. Schreibe sie auf.
Suche im Kapitel *Vegetables and fruit* drei Nomen. Schreibe sie auf.
Suche im Kapitel *At School* drei Verben. Schreibe sie auf.
Suche auf S. 112/113 drei Präpositionen und schreibe sie auf.

Finde das Kapitel *Colours and numbers*. Wie fragst du nach einer Telefonnummer?
Finde das Kapitel *Body and feelings*. Wie sagst du auf Englisch, dass du müde bist?
Finde das Kapitel *Lunch*. Wie bestellst du auf Englisch einen Hamburger?

Schlage S. 110/111 auf. Finde das Gegenteil zu folgenden Adjektiven und schreibe sie auf: cold, small, fit.
Finde das Kapitel *At home* und höre dir den Kangaroo's-Action-Rhyme an.

Jedes Wort in den Bildern kannst du dir vorlesen lassen, indem du es mit dem Hörstift antippst.

Zu Beginn solltest du dir immer alles erst einmal durchlesen und anhören.

Read and listen.

Listen to the song and sing:

The happy kangaroo song

Alle Aufträge unter dem Wimmelbild werden dir vorgelesen, wenn du sie antippst.

Dieses Symbol zeigt dir jeweils an, dass du dir hier ein Lied oder einen Reim anhören kannst, wenn du es antippst.

Wenn du eine Sprechblase antippst, wird dir der Text darin vorgelesen.

Hello

Do you speak English?

I like my bike.

letterbox

car

bike

Wenn du dieses Symbol in den Bildern findest, wird dir die Schrift in dem Bild vorgelesen, wenn du das Symbol antippst.

postman

girl

parcel

Find the letterbox.

Where is the girl in the wheelchair?

Find the car.

Where is the red ball?

Find Sally.

Am Ende steht immer der Auftrag, Sally zu suchen. Tippe zunächst den Suchauftrag an und finde dann Sally, die sich im Wimmelbild versteckt hat.

Mit diesem Symbol sind Suchaufträge gekennzeichnet. Tippe sie zunächst an und lass sie dir vorlesen. Dann kannst du sie mit deinem Hörstift lösen.

Hier findest du wichtige Wörter zum Thema des Kapitels in alphabetischer Reihenfolge.

Das ist die Wörterliste Englisch – Deutsch.

Nomen sind blau.

Adjektive sind grün.

Verben sind rot.

Wenn du die Sprechblasen antippst, liest sie dir der Hörstift vor.

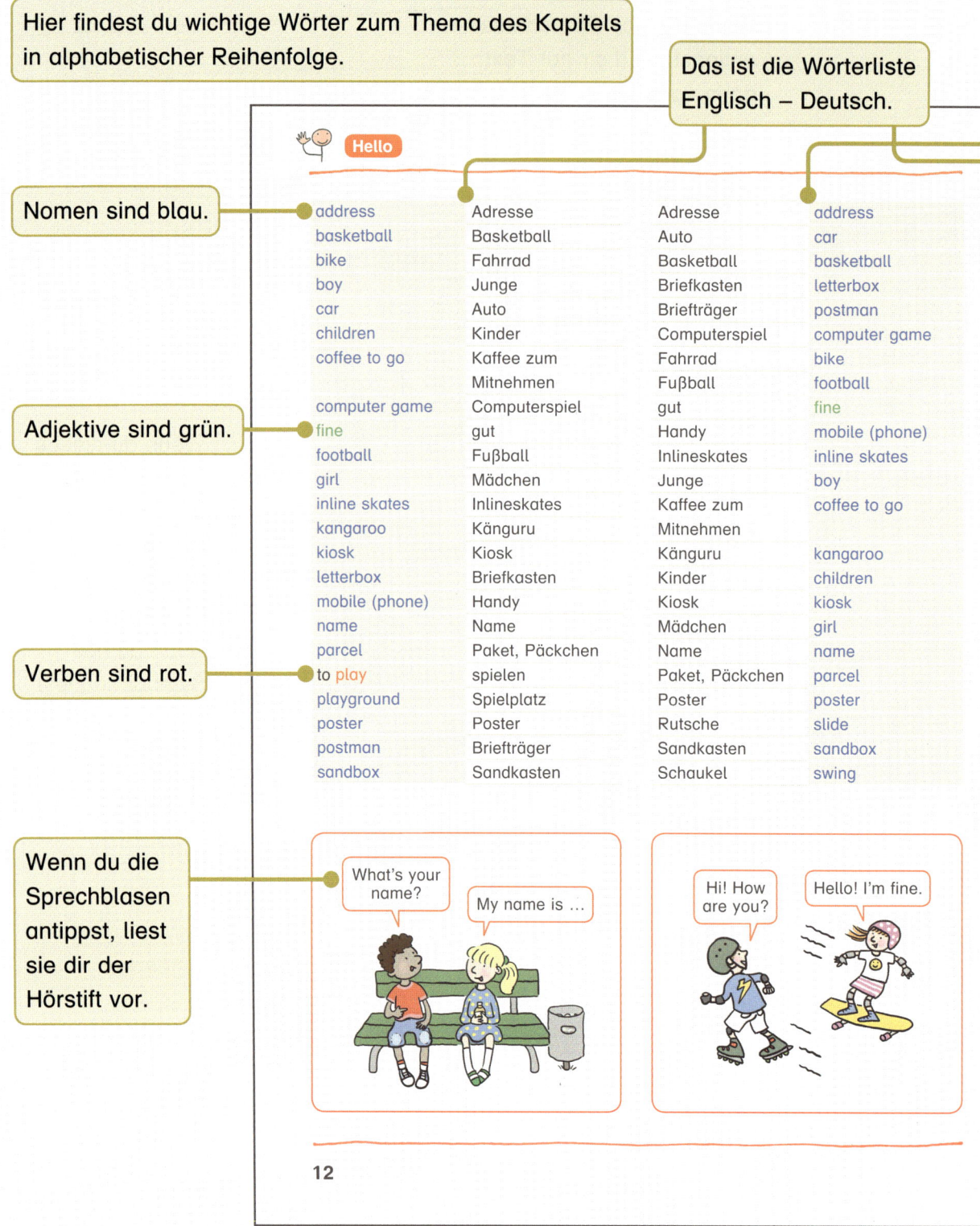

Hello

address	Adresse	Adresse	address
basketball	Basketball	Auto	car
bike	Fahrrad	Basketball	basketball
boy	Junge	Briefkasten	letterbox
car	Auto	Briefträger	postman
children	Kinder	Computerspiel	computer game
coffee to go	Kaffee zum Mitnehmen	Fahrrad	bike
		Fußball	football
computer game	Computerspiel	gut	fine
fine	gut	Handy	mobile (phone)
football	Fußball	Inlineskates	inline skates
girl	Mädchen	Junge	boy
inline skates	Inlineskates	Kaffee zum Mitnehmen	coffee to go
kangaroo	Känguru		
kiosk	Kiosk	Känguru	kangaroo
letterbox	Briefkasten	Kinder	children
mobile (phone)	Handy	Kiosk	kiosk
name	Name	Mädchen	girl
parcel	Paket, Päckchen	Name	name
to play	spielen	Paket, Päckchen	parcel
playground	Spielplatz	Poster	poster
poster	Poster	Rutsche	slide
postman	Briefträger	Sandkasten	sandbox
sandbox	Sandkasten	Schaukel	swing

What's your name?

My name is …

Hi! How are you?

Hello! I'm fine.

12

8

Das ist die Wörterliste Deutsch – Englisch.

Hello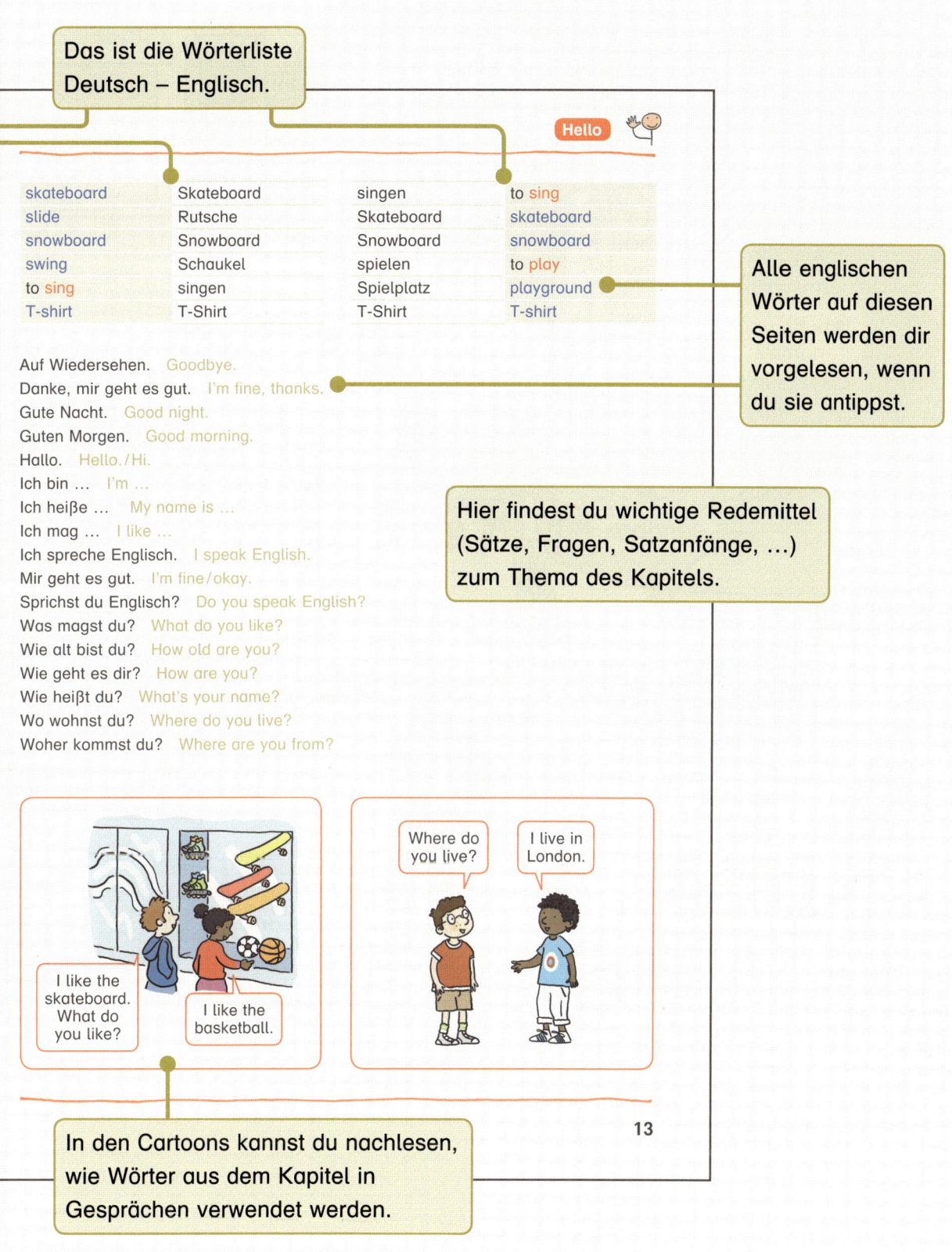

skateboard	Skateboard	singen	to sing
slide	Rutsche	Skateboard	skateboard
snowboard	Snowboard	Snowboard	snowboard
swing	Schaukel	spielen	to play
to sing	singen	Spielplatz	playground
T-shirt	T-Shirt	T-Shirt	T-shirt

Alle englischen Wörter auf diesen Seiten werden dir vorgelesen, wenn du sie antippst.

Auf Wiedersehen.   Goodbye.
Danke, mir geht es gut.   I'm fine, thanks.
Gute Nacht.   Good night.
Guten Morgen.   Good morning.
Hallo.   Hello./Hi.
Ich bin ...   I'm ...
Ich heiße ...   My name is ...
Ich mag ...   I like ...
Ich spreche Englisch.   I speak English.
Mir geht es gut.   I'm fine/okay.
Sprichst du Englisch?   Do you speak English?
Was magst du?   What do you like?
Wie alt bist du?   How old are you?
Wie geht es dir?   How are you?
Wie heißt du?   What's your name?
Wo wohnst du?   Where do you live?
Woher kommst du?   Where are you from?

Hier findest du wichtige Redemittel (Sätze, Fragen, Satzanfänge, ...) zum Thema des Kapitels.

I like the skateboard. What do you like?

I like the basketball.

Where do you live?

I live in London.

13

In den Cartoons kannst du nachlesen, wie Wörter aus dem Kapitel in Gesprächen verwendet werden.

9

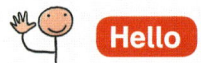

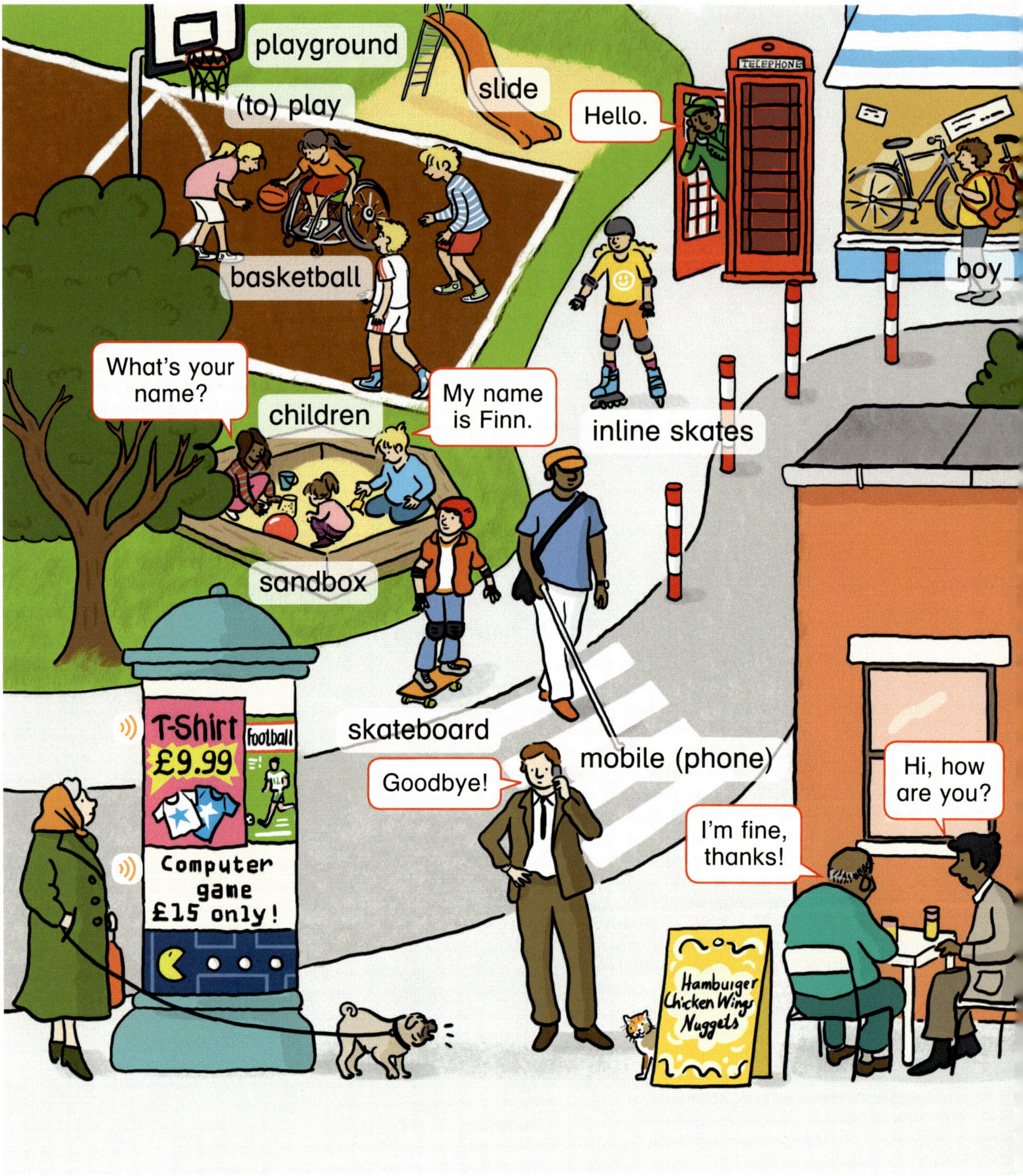
playground
slide
(to) play
Hello.
TELEPHONE
basketball
boy
What's your name?
children
My name is Finn.
inline skates
sandbox
T-Shirt £9.99
football
Computer game £15 only!
skateboard
mobile (phone)
Goodbye!
Hi, how are you?
I'm fine, thanks!
Hamburger
Chicken Wings
Nuggets

Read and listen.

Listen to the song and sing:

The happy kangaroo song

Do you speak English?

I like my bike.

bike shop

letterbox

bike

car

SnackBar

Cake

Hot Dog

KIOSK

Coffee to go ??

OPEN

postman

girl

To
H. Miller name
21 Main Street
London TW 13
UK

parcel

? Find the letterbox.

? Where is the girl in the wheelchair?

? Find the car.

? Where is the red ball?

? Find Sally.

address	Adresse	Adresse	address
basketball	Basketball	Auto	car
bike	Fahrrad	Basketball	basketball
boy	Junge	Briefkasten	letterbox
car	Auto	Briefträger	postman
children	Kinder	Computerspiel	computer game
coffee to go	Kaffee zum Mitnehmen	Fahrrad	bike
		Fußball	football
computer game	Computerspiel	gut	fine
fine	gut	Handy	mobile (phone)
football	Fußball	Inlineskates	inline skates
girl	Mädchen	Junge	boy
inline skates	Inlineskates	Kaffee zum Mitnehmen	coffee to go
kangaroo	Känguru		
kiosk	Kiosk	Känguru	kangaroo
letterbox	Briefkasten	Kinder	children
mobile (phone)	Handy	Kiosk	kiosk
name	Name	Mädchen	girl
parcel	Paket, Päckchen	Name	name
to play	spielen	Paket, Päckchen	parcel
playground	Spielplatz	Poster	poster
poster	Poster	Rutsche	slide
postman	Briefträger	Sandkasten	sandbox
sandbox	Sandkasten	Schaukel	swing

to sing	singen	singen	to sing
skateboard	Skateboard	Skateboard	skateboard
slide	Rutsche	Snowboard	snowboard
snowboard	Snowboard	spielen	to play
swing	Schaukel	Spielplatz	playground
T-shirt	T-Shirt	T-Shirt	T-shirt

Auf Wiedersehen.   Goodbye.

Danke, mir geht es gut.   I'm fine, thanks.

Gute Nacht.   Good night.

Guten Morgen.   Good morning.

Hallo.   Hello./Hi.

Ich bin …   I'm …

Ich heiße …   My name is …

Ich mag …   I like …

Ich spreche Englisch.   I speak English.

Mir geht es gut.   I'm fine/okay.

Sprichst du Englisch?   Do you speak English?

Was magst du?   What do you like?

Wie alt bist du?   How old are you?

Wie geht es dir?   How are you?

Wie heißt du?   What's your name?

Wo wohnst du?   Where do you live?

Woher kommst du?   Where are you from?

13

Read and listen.

Listen to the songs and sing:

The colour song

The 100 kangaroos song

Listen to the rhyme:

Sally's rhyme

80

CIRCUS
90

100

green

seven 7

Flowers

Blackstreet

eight 8

white

nine 9

10

black

ten

eleven 11

twelve 12

nineteen

Greenmeadow

twenty 20

19

pink

ighteen

18

red

? Find the orange house.

? Where is the yellow waggon?

? Which house is red?

? Who wears a blue dress?

? Tap the purple part of the rainbow.

? Find number 100.

? Tap number 1.

? Find Sally.

beige	beige	ausmalen	to colour
black	schwarz	beige	beige
blue	blau	blau	blue
bronze	bronzen, Bronze	braun	brown
brown	braun	bronzen, Bronze	bronze
colour	Farbe	bunt	colourful
to colour	ausmalen	dunkel	dark
coloured	farbig	dunkelblau	dark blue
colourful	bunt	Farbe	colour
to count	zählen	farbig	coloured
to count backwards	rückwärts zählen	gelb	yellow
to count forward	vorwärts zählen	golden, Gold	gold
to count from …	von … nach …	grau	grey
to …	zählen	grün	green
dark	dunkel	Haus	house
dark blue	dunkelblau	hell	light
to draw	zeichnen	hellblau	light blue
gold	golden, Gold	leuchten	to shine
green	grün	leuchtend	shiny
grey	grau	lila	purple
house	Haus	malen	to paint
light	hell	orange	orange
light blue	hellblau	Regenbogen	rainbow
number	Zahl	rosa, pink	pink
orange	orange	rot	red
to paint	malen	rückwärts zählen	to count backwards
pink	rosa, pink	schwarz	black
purple	lila	silbern, Silber	silver
rainbow	Regenbogen	violett	violet
red	rot	von … nach …	to count from …
to shine	leuchten	zählen	to …
shiny	leuchtend	vorwärts zählen	to count forward
silver	silbern, Silber	Wagen	waggon
train	Zug	weiß	white
violet	violett	Zahl	number
waggon	Wagen	zählen	to count
white	weiß	zeichnen	to draw
yellow	gelb	Zug	train

1	one	11	eleven	30	thirty		
2	two	12	twelve	40	forty		
3	three	13	thirteen	50	fifty		
4	four	14	fourteen	60	sixty		
5	five	15	fifteen	70	seventy		
6	six	16	sixteen	80	eighty		
7	seven	17	seventeen	90	ninety		
8	eight	18	eighteen	100	hundred		
9	nine	19	nineteen	1000	thousand		
10	ten	20	twenty	1000000	million		

Die (Bälle, …) sind (rot, …)   The (balls, …) are (red, …)

Die Farbe von …   The colour of …

Es ist (grün, …).   It's (green, …)

Welche Farbe hat/haben die …?   What colour is/are the …?

Welche Farbe hat es?   What colour is it?

Was ist deine Lieblingsfarbe?   What's your favourite colour?

Meine Lieblingsfarbe ist …   My favourite colour is …

Ich mag … (am liebsten).   I like … (best).

Wie alt bist du?   How old are you?

Ich bin … Jahre alt.   I'm … years old.

Wie lautet deine Telefonnummer?   What's your telephone number?

Meine Telefonnummer ist …   My telephone number is …

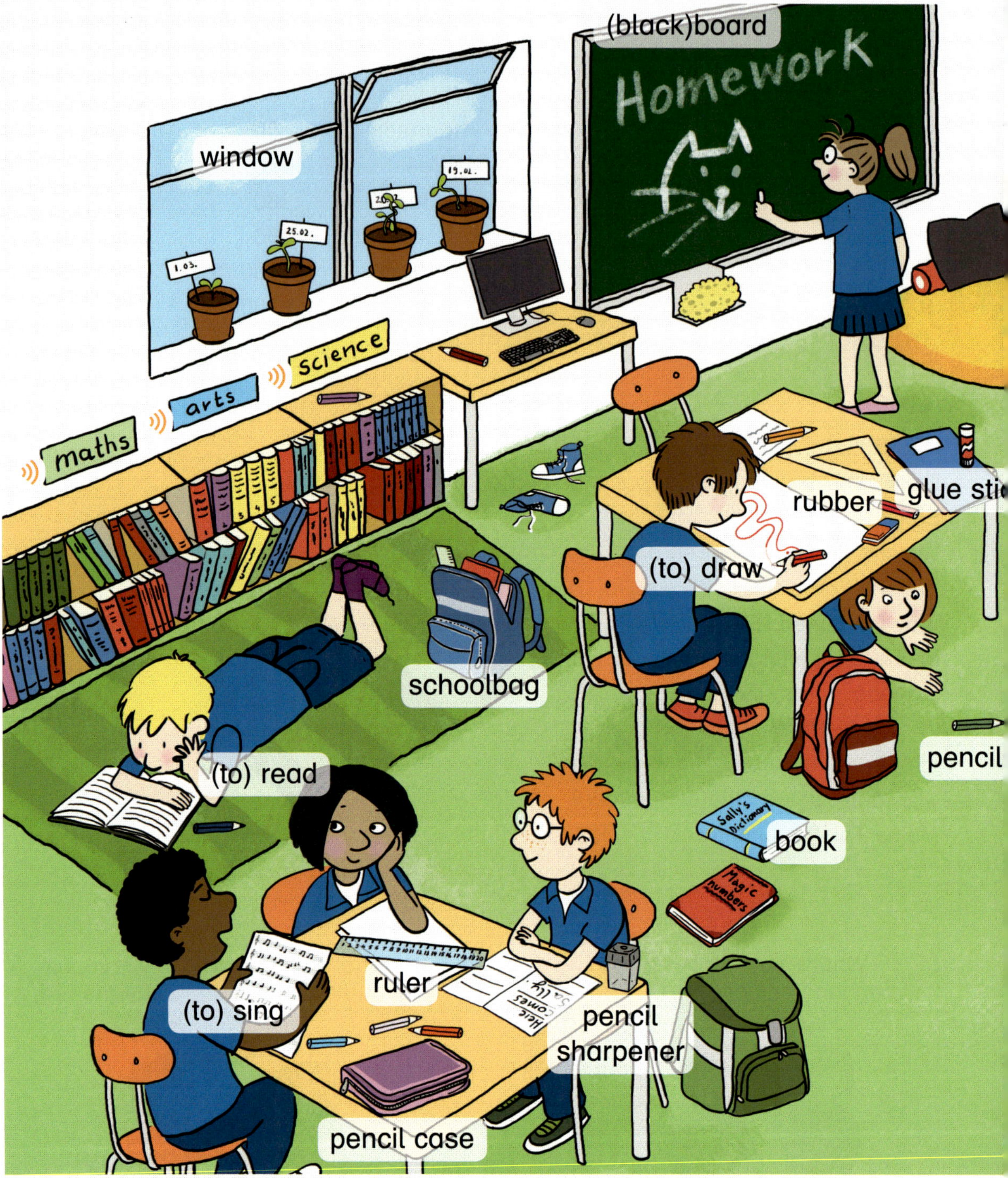

(black)board

Homework

window

science

arts

maths

rubber

glue stick

(to) draw

schoolbag

pencil

(to) read

book

ruler

(to) sing

pencil sharpener

pencil case

Read and listen.

Listen to the rhyme:

Alphabet rhyme

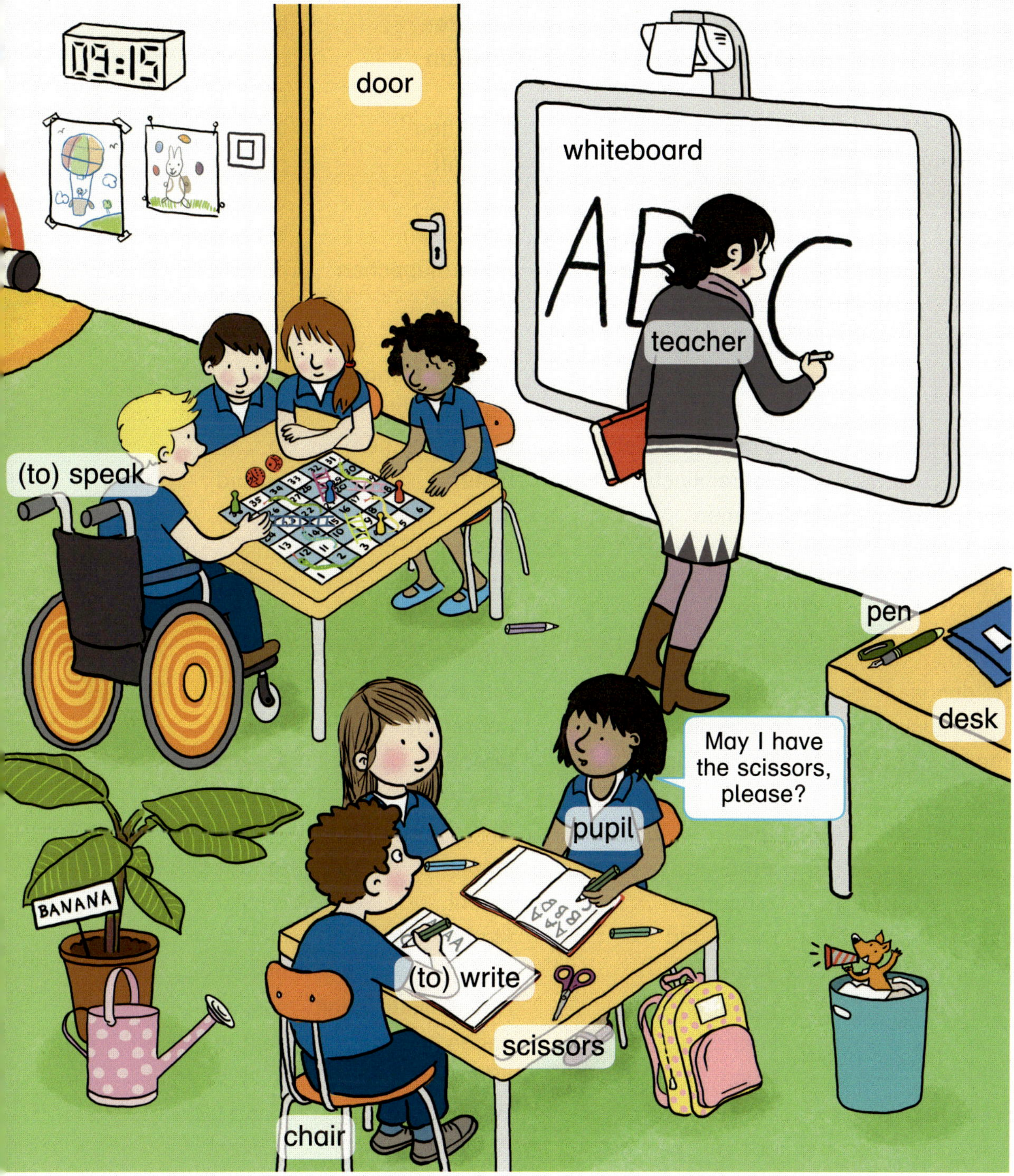
09:15
door
whiteboard
ABC
teacher
(to) speak
pen
desk
May I have the scissors, please?
pupil
BANANA
(to) write
scissors
chair

- Find the girl with glasses.
- Tap the ruler on the desk.
- Where is the blue schoolbag?
- Tap the pupil under the desk.
- Who is reading?
- Find Sally.

arts	Kunstunterricht	abhaken	to tick
assembly	Versammlung	arbeiten	to work
behind	hinter	auf	on
bell	Glocke, Gong	ausfüllen	to fill in
between	zwischen	Bleistift	pencil
(black)board	Tafel	Buch	book
book	Buch	einkreisen	to circle
to break	Pause machen	Federmäppchen	pencil case
chair	Stuhl	Fenster	window
chalk	Kreide	Füller	pen
to circle	einkreisen	Glocke, Gong	bell
class	Klasse	Hausaufgabe	homework
classroom	Klassenzimmer	herausnehmen	to take out
desk	Schreibtisch	hinter	behind
to do maths	rechnen	in	in
to do sports	Sport treiben	Klasse	class
door	Tür	Klassenzimmer	classroom
to draw	zeichnen	Klebestift	glue stick
to fill in	ausfüllen	Kreide	chalk
folder	Schnellhefter	Kunstunterricht	arts
glue stick	Klebestift	Lehrer(in)	teacher
homework	Hausaufgabe	lernen	to learn
in	in	Lesen und	literacy
in front of	vor	Schreiben	
to learn	lernen	lesen	to read
to listen	zuhören	Lineal	ruler
literacy	Lesen und	Mathe	maths
	Schreiben	Musik	music
to match	zuordnen	Naturwissenschaft	science
maths	Mathe	neben	next to
music	Musik	öffnen	to open
next to	neben	Papierkorb	waste-paper basket
on	auf	Pause machen	to break
to open	öffnen	Pausenhof	playground
pen	Füller	Radiergummi	rubber
pencil	Bleistift	rechnen	to do maths
pencil case	Federmäppchen	Schere	scissors

pencil sharpener	Spitzer	Schnellhefter	folder
to play	spielen	schreiben	to write
playground	Pausenhof	Schreibtisch	desk
pupil	Schüler(in)	Schule	school
to put away	wegräumen	Schüler(in)	pupil
to read	lesen	Schulfach	school subject
rubber	Radiergummi	Schulhof	schoolyard
ruler	Lineal	Schulsachen	school things
school	Schule	Schultasche	schoolbag
school subject	Schulfach	Schuluniform	school uniform
school things	Schulsachen	singen	to sing
school uniform	Schuluniform	spielen	to play
schoolbag	Schultasche	Spitzer	pencil sharpener
schoolyard	Schulhof	Sport	sports
science	Naturwissenschaft	Sport treiben	to do sports
scissors	Schere	sprechen	to speak
to sing	singen	Stuhl	chair
to speak	sprechen	Tafel	(black)board
sports	Sport	Tür	door
to take out	herausnehmen	unter	under
teacher	Lehrer(in)	Versammlung	assembly
to tick	abhaken	vor	in front of
under	unter	wegräumen	to put away
waste-paper basket	Papierkorb	Whiteboard	whiteboard
whiteboard	Whiteboard	zeichnen	to draw
window	Fenster	zuhören	to listen
to work	arbeiten	zuordnen	to match
to write	schreiben	zwischen	between

Ich bin in der Klasse …/… Schule.   I'm in class …/… school.

Ich habe ein(e, en) …   I've got a …

Ich habe mein(e, en) … vergessen.   I don't have my …

Kann ich … haben?   Can I have …?

Kann ich bitte zur Toilette gehen?   Can I go to the toilet, please?

Meine Lehrerin/Mein Lehrer heißt Frau/Herr …   My teacher is Mrs/Mr …

Wo ist mein(e)/dein(e) …?   Where is my/your …?

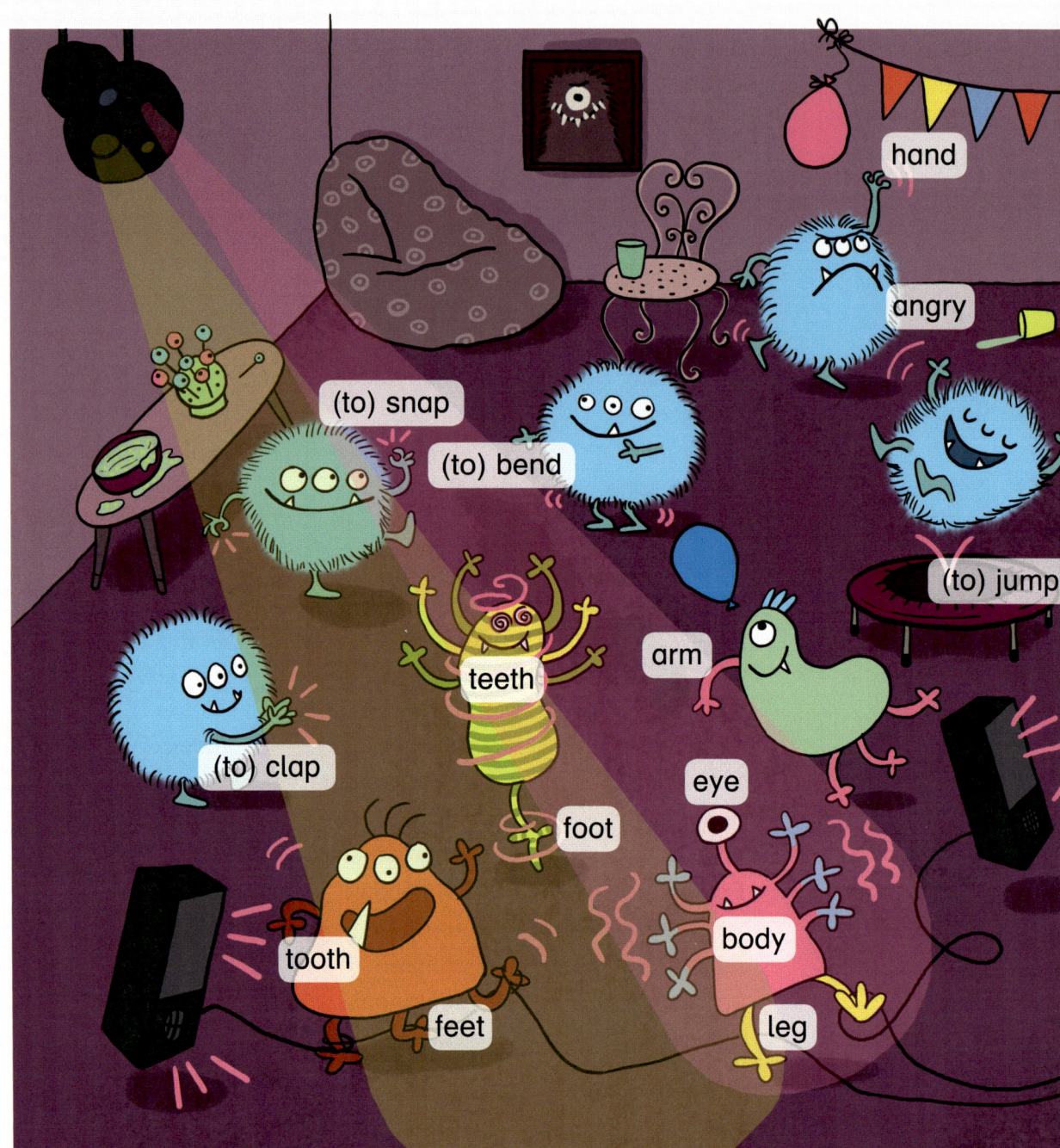

hand

angry

(to) snap

(to) bend

(to) jump

teeth

arm

(to) clap

eye

foot

tooth

body

feet

leg

🎧 Read and listen.

Listen to the songs and sing:

🎵 Head and shoulders

🎵 If you're happy

❓ Tap the monster with only one arm, three legs and one eye.

❓ Where is the monster with two eyes, two arms and one ear?

❓ Tap the scared monster.

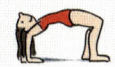

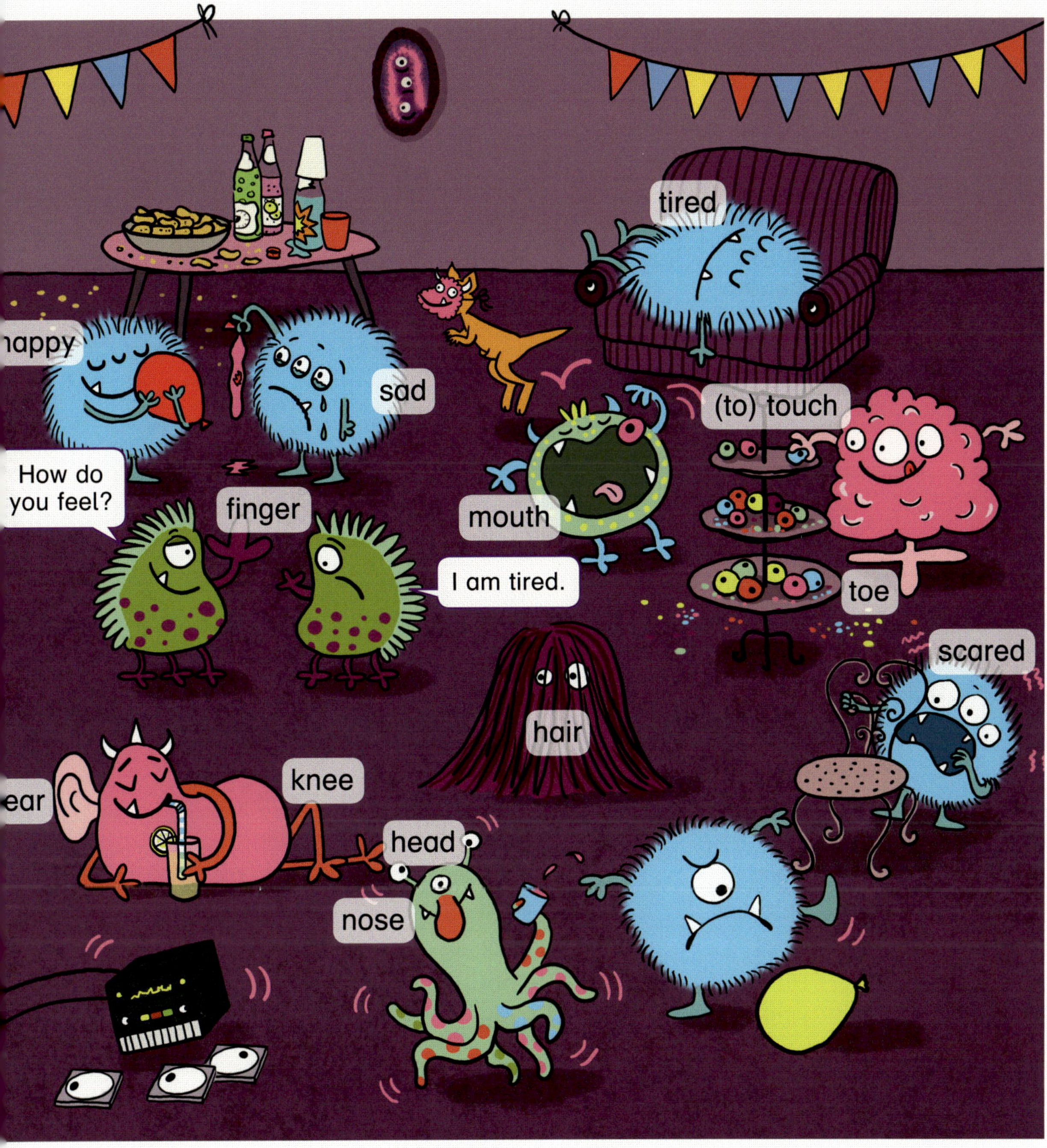
tired
happy
sad
(to) touch
How do you feel?
finger
mouth
I am tired.
toe
scared
hair
knee
ear
head
nose

- Find the monster snapping its fingers.
- Which monster has six arms but only one eye?
- Tap the sad monster.
- Tap the angry monster with one eye.
- Find Sally.

angry	wütend, zornig	Arm	arm
ankle	Knöchel	Auge	eye
arm	Arm	Augenbraue	eyebrow
belly	Bauch	Bauch	belly
belly button	Bauchnabel	Bauchnabel	belly button
to bend	beugen	Bein	leg
body	Körper	berühren	to touch
brain	Gehirn	beugen	to bend
cheeks	Wangen	Ellbogen	elbow
chin	Kinn	Finger	finger
to clap	klatschen	Fingernagel	fingernail
ear	Ohr	Fuß, Füße	foot, feet
elbow	Ellbogen	Gehirn	brain
eye	Auge	Gesicht	face
eyebrow	Augenbraue	glücklich	happy
eyelashes	Wimpern	gut	fine
face	Gesicht	Haar	hair
fine	gut	Hals	neck
finger	Finger	Hand	hand
fingernail	Fingernagel	Herz	heart
foot, feet	Fuß, Füße	Hüfte	hip
forehead	Stirn	hungrig	hungry
hair	Haar	Kinn	chin
hand	Hand	klatschen	to clap
happy	glücklich	Knie	knee
head	Kopf	Knöchel	ankle
heart	Herz	Kopf	head
hip	Hüfte	Körper	body
hungry	hungrig	müde	tired
to jump	springen	Mund	mouth
knee	Knie	Nase	nose
leg	Bein	Oberschenkel	thigh
mouth	Mund	Ohr	ear
neck	Hals	(mit den Fingern) schnippen	to snap (your fingers)
nose	Nase	Schulter	shoulder
sad	traurig		

scared	verängstigt, erschrocken	schütteln	to shake
to shake	schütteln	springen	to jump
shoulder	Schulter	stampfen	to stamp
to snap (your fingers)	mit den Fingern schnippen	Stirn	forehead
to stamp	stampfen	traurig	sad
thigh	Oberschenkel	verängstigt, erschrocken	scared
tired	müde	Wangen	cheeks
toe	Zeh	Wimpern	eyelashes
toenail	Zehennagel	wütend, zornig	angry
tooth, teeth	Zahn, Zähne	Zahn, Zähne	tooth, teeth
to touch	berühren	Zeh	toe
		Zehennagel	toenail

Wie fühlst du dich? How do you feel?
Ich bin glücklich/traurig/… I'm happy/sad/…
Wie geht es dir? How are you?
Mir geht es gut. I'm fine./I'm okay.
Klatsche in die Hände. Clap your hands.
Schnippe mit den Fingern. Snap your fingers.
Berühre dein(e) … Touch your …
Beuge dein(e) … Bend your …

It's 5 pounds.

How much is the basketball?

inline skates

£25

racing car

spaceship

£3

£8

£5.60

£2,30

TETRIX DS

£11

£6,80

£5

stickers

90 P

20 P

computer game

horse

£3

teddy bear

helicopter

£5

£3

castle

£12

doll

car

£4,30

£4

guitar

£25

£1

Read and listen.

Listen to the song and sing:

A little ball, a big ball

Listen to the rhyme:

Fuzzy Wuzzy

Tap the teddy bears.

Find the coins on the floor.

Where is the green helmet?

Find the toy that costs one pound.

What is it? Listen to the price and tap the correct thing.

- ❓ It's 40 pounds.
- ❓ It's 11 pounds.
- ❓ It's 4 pounds 30 pence.
- ❓ It's 80 pence.
- ❓ It's 20 pence.
- ❓ Find Sally.

ball	Ball	Aufkleber	stickers
basketball	Basketball	Auto	car
big	groß	Ball	ball
bike	Fahrrad	Basketball	basketball
board game	Brettspiel	Brettspiel	board game
book	Buch	Buch	book
car	Auto	Burg	castle
castle	Burg	Computerspiel	computer game
computer game	Computerspiel	Dollar	dollar
cuddly toy	Kuscheltier	Euro	euro
doll	Puppe	Fahrrad	bike
dollar	Dollar	ferngesteuertes Auto	remote controlled car
euro	Euro	Frisbee	frisbee
football	Fußball	Fußball	football
frisbee	Frisbee	Geld	money
guitar	Gitarre	Gitarre	guitar
helicopter	Hubschrauber	groß	big
helmet	Helm	Helm	helmet
horse	Pferd	Hubschrauber	helicopter
inline skates	Inlineskates	Inlineskates	inline skates
money	Geld	klein	small
MP4 player	MP4-Player	Kuscheltier	cuddly toy
pence	Pence	MP4-Player	MP4 player
pencils	Stifte	Pence	pence
penny	Penny		

I want the doll.

It's 3 pounds.

How much is the book?

It's 1 pound, 50 pence.

playing cards	Spielkarten	Penny	penny
pound	Pfund	Pferd	horse
racing car	Rennauto	Pfund	pound
remote controlled car	ferngesteuertes Auto	Puppe	doll
		Raumschiff	spaceship
scooter	Roller	Rennauto	racing car
skateboard	Skateboard	Roller	scooter
skipping rope	Springseil	Skateboard	skateboard
small	klein	Smartphone	smartphone
smartphone	Smartphone	Spielkarten	playing cards
spaceship	Raumschiff	Springseil	skipping rope
stickers	Aufkleber	Stelzen	stilts
stilts	Stelzen	Stifte	pencils
tablet	Tablet	Tablet	tablet
teddy bear	Teddybär	Teddybär	teddy bear
to want	wollen	wollen	to want
to wish (for)	sich wünschen	sich wünschen	to wish (for)

Wie viel kostet der (die, das) …?   How much is the …?
Der (die, das) … kostet … Pfund.   The … is … pounds.
Es kostet … Pfund.   It's … pounds.
Ich hätte gern/Ich möchte …   I'd like/I would like …
Ich will …   I want …
Er/Sie will …   He/She wants …

I'd like a new bike.

I've got a big teddy bear.

I've got a small teddy bear.

scarf

coat

cap

pullover

jacket

a pair of trousers

shorts

shoes

socks

jeans

T-shirt

gloves

boots

 Read and listen.

Listen to the songs and sing:

 Black socks

The clothes song

shirt

I take off the pullover.

I put on the jacket.

pyjamas

Look, he's wearing a blue jacket!

woolly hat

dress

skirt

❓ Tap the gloves.

❓ Tap the scarf.

❓ Tap the boots.

❓ Tap the pink dress.

❓ Find Sally.

Clothes

anorak	Anorak	Anorak	anorak
belt	Gürtel	anziehen	to put on
bikini	Bikini	aufhängen	to hang up
boots	Stiefel	ausziehen	to take off
button	Knopf	Badeanzug	swimsuit
cap	Kappe, Mütze	Badehose	swimming trunks
clothes	Kleidung	Bikini	bikini
coat	Mantel	falten	to fold
collar	Kragen	Gummistiefel	wellies (wellingtons)
dress	Kleid		
to fold	falten	Gürtel	belt
gloves	Handschuhe	Handschuhe	gloves
to hang up	aufhängen	Hemd	shirt
hood	Kapuze	Hose	a pair of trousers
hoodie	Kapuzenpullover	Jacke	jacket
jacket	Jacke	Jeans	jeans
jeans	Jeans	Jogginganzug	jogging suit
jogging suit	Jogginganzug	Kappe, Mütze	cap
jumpsuit	Overall	Kapuze	hood
a pair of	ein Paar	Kapuzenpullover	hoodie
a pair of trousers	Hose	Kleid	dress
pullover	Pullover	Kleidung	clothes
to put on	anziehen	Knopf	button
pyjamas	Schlafanzug	Kragen	collar
raincoat	Regenmantel	Krawatte	tie
sandals	Sandalen	Mantel	coat
scarf	Schal	Mütze	woolly hat, cap
shirt	Hemd	Overall	jumpsuit
shoes	Schuhe	ein Paar	a pair of
shorts	Shorts	Pulli	sweater, jumper
skirt	Rock	Pullover	pullover
sneakers, trainers	Turnschuhe	Regenmantel	raincoat
socks	Socken	Reißverschluss	zipper
sweater, jumper	Pulli	Rock	skirt
swimming trunks	Badehose	Sandalen	sandals
swimsuit	Badeanzug	Schal	scarf
to take off	ausziehen	Schlafanzug	pyjamas

tie	Krawatte	Schuhe	shoes
tights	Strumpfhose	Shorts	shorts
T-shirt	T-Shirt	Socken	socks
underwear	Unterwäsche	Stiefel	boots
vest	Weste	Strumpfhose	tights
to wash	waschen	tragen	to wear
to wear	tragen	T-Shirt	T-shirt
wellies (wellingtons)	Gummistiefel	Turnschuhe	sneakers, trainers
		Unterwäsche	underwear
woolly hat, cap	Mütze	waschen	to wash
zipper	Reißverschluss	Weste	vest

Ich ziehe mein/ein … an.   I put on my/a …

Ich ziehe mein … aus.   I take off my …

Ich habe … an.   I'm wearing …

Was hat er/sie an?   What is he/she wearing?

Er/Sie hat … an.   He/She is wearing …

Sie zieht ihr … an.   She puts on her …

Sie zieht ihr … aus.   She takes off her …

Wie passt es?   How does it fit?

Es passt.   It fits.

Es/Er/Sie ist zu groß.   It's too big.

Es/Er/Sie ist zu klein.   It's too small.

Welche Größe ist es?   What size is it?

Es ist Größe S/M/L.   It's a small/medium/large.

Does it fit?

No, it's too big.

Do you like it?

Yes, I like the colour.

snowy

cloud

cold

rainbow

rainy

windy

cloudy

foggy

thunderstorm

sun

warm

sunny

Read and listen.

Listen to the songs and sing:

Sally's week

Incy wincy spider

It's hot today!

10:00
London
5°
Monday today

Tuesday 10°
Wednesday 12°
Thursday 8°
Friday 7°
Saturday 4°
Sunday 0°

Find the girl with the sunglasses.

Tap the snowman.

What day is it today?

Where is it foggy?

When is it rainy?

Find Sally.

35

calendar	Kalender	(auf)blitzen	to flash
cloud	Wolke	Blitz	lightning
cloudy	wolkig	Donner	thunder
cold	kalt	donnern	to thunder
day	Tag	eisig	icy
days of the week	Wochentage	gestern	yesterday
dry	trocken	Gewitter	thunderstorm
to flash	(auf)blitzen	heiß	hot
fog	Nebel	heute	today
foggy	neblig	Himmel	sky
heat	Hitze	Hitze	heat
hot	heiß	Kalender	calendar
hurricane	Wirbelsturm	kalt	cold
icy	eisig	Landkarte	map
lightning	Blitz	morgen	tomorrow
map	Landkarte	nass	wet
rain	Regen	Nebel	fog
to rain	regnen	neblig	foggy
rainbow	Regenbogen	Regen	rain
rainy	regnerisch	Regenbogen	rainbow
to shine	scheinen	regnen	to rain
sky	Himmel	regnerisch	rainy
snow	Schnee	scheinen	to shine
to snow	schneien	Schnee	snow
snowy	verschneit	schneien	to snow
storm	Sturm	Sonne	sun
to storm	stürmen	sonnig	sunny
sun	Sonne	Sturm	storm
sunny	sonnig	stürmen	to storm
temperature	Temperatur	Tag	day
thunder	Donner	Temperatur	temperature
to thunder	donnern	trocken	dry
thunderstorm	Gewitter	verschneit	snowy
today	heute	warm	warm
tomorrow	morgen	Wetter	weather
warm	warm	Wettervorhersage	weather forecast
weather	Wetter	Wind	wind

weather forecast	Wettervorhersage	windig	windy
week	Woche	Wirbelsturm	hurricane
weekend	Wochenende	Woche	week
wet	nass	Wochenende	weekend
wind	Wind	Wochentage	days of the week
windy	windig	Wolke	cloud
yesterday	gestern	wolkig	cloudy

Monday	Montag
Tuesday	Dienstag
Wednesday	Mittwoch
Thursday	Donnerstag
Friday	Freitag
Saturday	Samstag
Sunday	Sonntag

Welchen Tag haben wir?   What day is it?
Heute ist …   Today is …
Wie ist das Wetter?   What's the weather like?
Es ist kalt.   It's cold.
Es ist regnerisch.   It's rainy.
Es ist sonnig.   It's sunny.

What's the weather like today?

It's sunny and warm.

What day is it?

It's Wednesday.

winter

crown

December

Christmas

January

snowman

February

card

Valentine's Day

calendar

November

Happy Thanksgiving!

turkey

October

jack-o'-lantern

September

kite

autumn

Read and listen.

Listen to the songs and sing:

Funny bunny hop

Cut the cake

Listen to the rhyme:

Five little Easter rabbits

))) **spring**

))) **March**

Easter bunny

Easter egg

basket

))) **April**

flowers

))) **May**

blossoms

))) **Birthday Calendar**

cake   present

Happy Birthday!

Jan Feb Mar Apr May June

5 Sally

10 Mum

16 Dad

Sept Oct Nov Dec   balloon

18 Fin

))) **August**

Summer holidays!

))) **July**

swimming pool

))) **June**

ice cream

))) **summer**

? Tap the girl in the swimming pool.

? Tap the Easter egg next to the basket.

? Tap the sun behind the tree.

? Tap 3 winter months.

? When is Sally's birthday?

? In which month is Valentine's Day?

? Find Sally.

39

autumn	Herbst	Blume	flower
blossom	Blüte	Blüte	blossom
calendar	Kalender	Drachen	kite
Christmas	Weihnachten	Eis	ice cream
Easter Monday	Ostermontag	Erntedankfest	Thanksgiving Day
Easter Sunday	Ostersonntag	Ferien	holidays
flower	Blume	Frühling	spring
Good Friday	Karfreitag	Herbst	autumn
holidays	Ferien	Jahr	year
ice cream	Eis	Jahreszeiten	seasons
jack-o'-lantern	Kürbislaterne	Kalender	calendar
kite	Drachen	Karfreitag	Good Friday
month	Monat	Kürbislaterne	jack-o'-lantern
seasons	Jahreszeiten	Monat	month
snowman	Schneemann	Ostermontag	Easter Monday
spring	Frühling	Ostersonntag	Easter Sunday
summer	Sommer	Schneemann	snowman
swimming pool	Schwimmbecken	Schwimmbecken	swimming pool
Thanksgiving Day	Erntedankfest	Sommer	summer
turkey	Truthahn	Truthahn	turkey
Valentine's Day	Valentinstag	Valentinstag	Valentine's Day
winter	Winter	Weihnachten	Christmas
year	Jahr	Winter	winter

Happy Easter	Frohe Ostern	Frohe Ostern	Happy Easter
basket	Korb	auf	on
behind	hinter	färben, anmalen	to colour
to colour	färben, anmalen	hinter	behind
Easter bunny	Osterhase	in	in
Easter egg	Osterei	Korb	basket
to hide	verstecken	neben	next to
in	in	Osterei	Easter egg
in front of	vor	Osterhase	Easter bunny
next to	neben	unter	under
on	auf	verstecken	to hide
under	unter	vor	in front of

Birthday	Geburtstag	Geburtstag	Birthday
balloon	Ballon	Ballon	balloon
cake	Kuchen	Einladung	invitation
candle	Kerze	Gast	guest
card	Karte	Geschenk	present
crown	Krone	Karte	card
guest	Gast	Kerze	candle
invitation	Einladung	Krone	crown
party	Party, Feier	Kuchen	cake
present	Geschenk	Party, Feier	party

Alles Gute zum Geburtstag!   Happy birthday!

Wie alt bist du?   How old are you?

Ich bin … Jahre alt.   I'm … years old.

Wann ist dein Geburtstag?   When's your birthday?

Mein Geburtstag ist am 5. März.   My birthday is on the 5th of March.

Mein Geburtstag ist im Januar/Februar/…   My birthday is in January/February/…

Frohen Valentinstag!/Frohe Ostern!/Frohes Thanksgiving!   Happy Valentine!/Happy Easter!/Happy Thanksgiving!

Ich mag dich.   I like you.

Ich liebe dich.   I love you.

Fröhliche Weihnachten und ein frohes neues Jahr!   Merry Christmas and a Happy New Year!

Komm zu meiner Feier!   Come to my party!

Lass uns … feiern.   Let's celebrate …

Which season do you like best?

I like summer best.

January	Januar
February	Februar
March	März
April	April
May	Mai
June	Juni
July	Juli
August	August
September	September
October	Oktober
November	November
December	Dezember

family tree

parents

mother

twins

Mummy!!!!

Happy birthday, Grandpa!

father

baby

sister

brother

Read and listen.

Listen to the rhymes:

♫ Family rhyme

♫ Some families

We are best friends!

aunt

grandfather

friend

uncle

grandmother

? Tap the grandmother.

? Who is grandpa's best friend?

? Whose birthday is it?

? Tap the parents.

? Find the baby.

? Find Sally.

aunt	Tante	alleinerziehende/r Mutter/Vater	single mum/dad
baby	Baby	Baby	baby
(best) friend	(beste/r) Freund/in	(beste/r) Freund/in	(best) friend
boy	Junge	Bruder	brother
brother	Bruder	Cousin/e	cousin
cousin	Cousin/e	Ehefrau	wife
dad, daddy	Papa	Ehemann	husband
daughter	Tochter	Ehepartner/in	spouse
dead	tot	Eltern	parents
divorced	geschieden	Familienmitglied	family member
family member	Familienmitglied	Freund/in	friend
family tree	Stammbaum	Freundschaft	friendship
father	Vater	geschieden	divorced
first name	Vorname	Geschwister	siblings
friend	Freund/in	Großeltern	grandparents
friendship	Freundschaft	Großmutter	grandmother
girl	Mädchen	Großvater	grandfather
godfather	Pate	Junge	boy
godmother	Patin	Lebensgefährte, Lebensgefährtin	partner
grandfather	Großvater	Mädchen	girl
grandma, granny	Oma	Mama	mum, mummy
grandmother	Großmutter	Mutter	mother
grandpa	Opa	Nachname	surname
grandparents	Großeltern		
great-grandmother	Urgroßmutter		

husband	Ehemann	Neffe	nephew
married	verheiratet	Nichte	niece
mother	Mutter	Oma	grandma, granny
mum, mummy	Mama	Onkel	uncle
nephew	Neffe	Opa	grandpa
nickname	Spitzname	Papa	dad, daddy
niece	Nichte	Pate	godfather
parents	Eltern	Patin	godmother
partner	Lebensgefährte, Lebensgefährtin	Schwester	sister
		Sohn	son
relatives	Verwandte	Spitzname	nickname
siblings	Geschwister	Stammbaum	family tree
single mum/dad	alleinerziehende/r Mutter/Vater	Stiefbruder	stepbrother
		Stiefmutter	stepmother
sister	Schwester	Stiefschwester	stepsister
son	Sohn	Stiefvater	stepfather
spouse	Ehepartner/in	Tante	aunt
stepbrother	Stiefbruder	Tochter	daughter
stepfather	Stiefvater	tot	dead
stepmother	Stiefmutter	Zwillinge	twins
stepsister	Stiefschwester	Urgroßmutter	great-grandmother
surname	Nachname	Vater	father
twins	Zwillinge	verheiratet	married
uncle	Onkel	Verwandte	rolatives
wife	Ehefrau	Vorname	first name

Hast du eine/n …?   Have you got a/any…?

Wie viele … hast du?   How many … have you got?

Ich habe … (einen Bruder, …).   I have got/I've got … (a brother, …).

Ich habe keine … (Schwester, …).   I haven't got … (a sister, …).

Wer ist dein(e) beste(r) Freund(in)?   Who is your best friend?

Mein(e) beste(r) Freund(in) ist …   My best friend is …

Wie ist sein/ihr Name?   What's his/her name?

Das ist mein(e) … (Cousin, …).   This is my … (cousin, …).

Das sind meine … (Schwestern, …).   These are my … (sisters, …).

Er ist/Sie ist mein(e) … (Cousin/Cousine, …).   He is (he's)/She is (she's) my … (cousin, …).

Mein(e) Papa/Mama lebt nicht bei uns.   My dad/mom doesn't live with us.

Can I help you?

I'd like a pineapple, please.

pineapple

melon

garlic

tomato   carrot   spinach   bean

lettuce

smoothie

Green smoothies

£1,50

potato

banana

cucumber

cherry   plum   apple   pepper   pumpkin

Read and listen.

Listen to the songs and sing:

Ice cream rock

Fruit, fruit, fruit

Courtyard Café

scoop

strawberry

Do you like green smoothies?

No, I don't.

onion

(to) drink

(to) eat

ICE cream

vanilla

chocolate

lemon

one scoop of ice cream £1

pear

How much is one scoop of ice cream?

Find the bananas.

Tap the pear.

Find the melons.

Which fruit does the ice cream man like?

Find Sally.

apple	Apfel	Ananas	pineapple
banana	Banane	Apfel	apple
basket	Korb	Banane	banana
bean	Bohne	Birne	pear
bitter	bitter	bitter	bitter
blackberry	Brombeere	Blaubeere	blueberry
blueberry	Blaubeere	Blumenkohl	cauliflower
broccoli	Brokkoli	Bohne	bean
cabbage	Kohl	Brokkoli	broccoli
carrot	Karotte	Brombeere	blackberry
cauliflower	Blumenkohl	durstig	thirsty
cherry	Kirsche	eingießen	to pour
chocolate	Schokolade	Eiskrem	ice cream
cold	kalt	Eiskremstand	ice cream stand
cream	Sahne	Eiskugel	scoop
cucumber	Gurke	Erbse	pea
currant	Johannisbeere	Erdbeere	strawberry
to cut	schneiden	essen	to eat
delicious	köstlich	Frucht, Obst	fruit
to drink	trinken	fruchtig	fruity
drinks stand	Getränkestand	Gemüse	vegetables
to eat	essen	Getränkestand	drinks stand
fruit	Frucht, Obst	Grünkohl	kale
fruity	fruchtig	Gurke	cucumber
garlic	Knoblauch	Himbeere	raspberry
grape	Traube	hungrig	hungry
hungry	hungrig	Johannisbeere	currant
ice cream	Eiskrem	kalt	cold
ice cream stand	Eiskremstand	Karotte	carrot
kale	Grünkohl	Kartoffel, Kartoffeln	potato, potatoes
kiwi	Kiwi	Kirsche	cherry
leek	Lauch	Kiwi	kiwi
lemon	Zitrone	Knoblauch	garlic
lettuce	Salat	Kohl	cabbage
market	Markt	Korb	basket
melon	Melone	köstlich	delicious
mushroom	Pilz	Kürbis	pumpkin

nut	Nuss	Lauch	leek
onion	Zwiebel	lecker	tasty
orange	Orange, Apfelsine	Markt	market
pea	Erbse	Melone	melon
pear	Birne	Nuss	nut
to peel	schälen	Orange, Apfelsine	orange
pepper	Paprika	Paprika	pepper
pineapple	Ananas	Pflaume	plum
plum	Pflaume	Pilz	mushroom
potato, potatoes	Kartoffel, Kartoffeln	probieren	to taste
to pour	eingießen	Radieschen	radish
pumpkin	Kürbis	Sahne	cream
radish	Radieschen	Salat	lettuce
raspberry	Himbeere	sauer	sour
scoop	Eiskugel	schälen	to peel
smoothie	Smoothie	schneiden	to cut
sour	sauer	Schokolade	chocolate
spinach	Spinat	Smoothie	smoothie
strawberry	Erdbeere	Spinat	spinach
sweet	süß	süß	sweet
to taste	probieren	Tomate, Tomaten	tomato, tomatoes
tasty	lecker	Traube	grape
thirsty	durstig	trinken	to drink
tomato, tomatoes	Tomate, Tomaten	Vanllle	vanilla
vanilla	Vanille	Wassermelone	watermelon
vegetables	Gemüse	Zitrone	lemon
watermelon	Wassermelone	Zwiebel	onion

Kann ich dir/euch/Ihnen helfen?   Can I help you?

Ich hätte gerne …   I'd like …

Was kostet es?   How much is it?

Das macht … Pfund.   That's … pounds.

Hier, bitte.   Here you are.

Magst du …?   Do you like …?

Ja./Nein.   Yes, I do./No, I don't.

Was ist dein Lieblings…?   What's your favourite …?

Mein Lieblings… ist …   My favourite … is …

Can I have the butter, please?

Yes, please.

cereal

glass

juice

spoon

cup

hot chocolate

bowl

sugar

cheese

salt

MILK

ham

knife

Read and listen.

Listen to the songs and sing:

The breakfast rap

I'm a little teapot

Find the salt and the milk.

Find the tea and the toast.

Find the hot chocolate and the bread.

COFFEE

HONEY

JAM

pepper

TOAST

orange juice

Would you like some tea?

Pass me the sugar, please.

Here you are.

butter

roll

mug

plate

egg

good morning

bread

smoothie

Jam

bacon

water

fork

? Who has a smoothie for breakfast?

? Who has orange juice for breakfast?

? Who has a roll for breakfast?

? Find Sally.

51

bacon	Speck	Becher	mug
baked beans	eingemachte Bohnen in Tomatensauce	Brot	bread
		Brötchen	roll
		Butter	butter
boiled egg	gekochtes Ei	Cornflakes	cornflakes
bowl	Schale	Ei	egg
bread	Brot	eingemachte Bohnen in Tomatensauce	baked beans
breakfast	Frühstück		
butter	Butter		
cereal	Getreideflocken	englisches Frühstück	traditional English breakfast
cheese	Käse	Frischkäse	cream cheese
chocolate milk, hot chocolate	kalter/heißer Kakao	Frühstück	breakfast
coffee	Kaffee	frühstücken	to have breakfast
continental breakfast	kontinentales, kleines Frühstück	Gabel	fork
		gekochtes Ei	boiled egg
cornflakes	Cornflakes	Getreideflocken	cereal
cream cheese	Frischkäse	Glas	glass
cup	Tasse	Haferbrei	porridge
egg	Ei	Honig	honey
fork	Gabel	Kaffee	coffee
fried egg	Spiegelei	kalter/heißer Kakao	chocolate milk, hot chocolate
glass	Glas		
ham	Schinken	Käse	cheese

What do you have for breakfast?

For breakfast I have hot chocolate and toast with jam.

Would you like some orange juice?

Yes, please.

to **have** breakfast	frühstücken	kontinentales, kleines Frühstück	continental breakfast
honey	Honig	Löffel	spoon
jam	Marmelade	Marmelade	jam
juice	Saft	Messer, Messer	knife, knives
knife, knives	Messer, Messer	Milch	milk
marmalade	Orangen-marmelade	Müsli	muesli
milk	Milch	Orangen-marmelade	marmalade
muesli	Müsli		
mug	Becher	Orangensaft	orange juice
orange juice	Orangensaft	Pfannkuchen	pancake
pancake	Pfannkuchen	Pfeffer	pepper
pepper	Pfeffer	Rührei	scrambled egg
plate	Teller	Saft	juice
porridge	Haferbrei	Salz	salt
roll	Brötchen	Schale	bowl
salt	Salz	Schinken	ham
scrambled egg	Rührei	Sirup	syrup
smoothie	Smoothie	Smoothie	smoothie
spoon	Löffel	Speck	bacon
sugar	Zucker	Spiegelei	fried egg
syrup	Sirup	Tasse	cup
tea	Tee	Tee	tea
toast	Toast	Teller	plate
traditional English breakfast	englisches Frühstück	Toast	toast
water	Wasser	Wasser	water
		Zucker	sugar

Was frühstückst du?   What do you have for breakfast?

Zum Frühstück esse/trinke ich …   For breakfast I have …

Magst du … (Zucker, …) in deinen … (Tee, …)?   Do you like (sugar) in your (tea)?

Ja./Nein.   Yes, I do./No, I don't.

Kann ich bitte die Butter haben?   Can I have the butter, please?

Bitte sehr.   You're welcome.

Möchtest du Tee?   Would you like some tea?

Ja, bitte./Nein, danke.   Yes, please./No, thank you.

Bitte reiche mir den Zucker.   Pass me the sugar, please.

Hier, bitte sehr.   Here you are.

fox

guinea pig

(to) feed

budgie

(to) moo

cow

butterfly

sheep

cat

goose

duck (to) croak

fish

Read and listen.

Listen to the songs and sing:

♪ Five little pets

♪ Old MacDonald has a farm

♪ Bingo song

Find the mouse under the tree.

Tap the cow.

Tap the fox.

Tap the sheep in the house.

Find the yellow fish.

(to) neigh

horse

(to) cluck

(to) bark

dog

(to) chirp

bird

pig

fly

(to) squeak

hen

bee

mouse

? Tap the white cat.

? Find the goose next to the pond.

? Where is the pig?

? Where are the budgies?

? Find the bee.

? Find Sally.

animal	Tier	Bauernhof	farm
animal centre	Tierheim	bellen	to bark
to bark	bellen	Biene	bee
beak	Schnabel	Eichhörnchen	squirrel
bee	Biene	Eier legen	to lay eggs
bird	Vogel	Ente	duck
budgie	Wellensittich	Esel	donkey
butterfly	Schmetterling	Feder	feather
cage	Käfig	Ferkel	piglet
cat	Katze	Fisch, Fische	fish, fish
chick	Küken	Fliege	fly
to chirp	zwitschern	fliegen	to fly
claw	Kralle	Flügel	wing
to cluck	gackern	Fohlen	foal
cow	Kuh	Frosch	frog
to croak	quaken	Fuchs	fox
dog	Hund	füttern	to feed
donkey	Esel	gackern	to cluck
duck	Ente	Gans, Gänse	goose, geese
farm	Bauernhof	Goldfisch	goldfish
feather	Feder	Hafer	oats
to feed	füttern	Hamster	hamster
fish, fish	Fisch, Fische	Haustier	pet
fly	Fliege	Heu	hay
to fly	fliegen	Huf, Hufe	hoof, hooves
foal	Fohlen	Huhn	hen
fox	Fuchs	Hund	dog
frog	Frosch	Käfig	cage
to give milk	Milch geben	Kaninchen	rabbit
goat	Ziege	Kätzchen	kitten
goldfish	Goldfisch	Katze	cat
goose, geese	Gans, Gänse	Kralle	claw
guinea pig	Meerschweinchen	Kuh	cow
hamster	Hamster	Küken	chick
hay	Heu	Landschildkröte	tortoise
hen	Huhn	Maus, Mäuse	mouse, mice
hoof, hooves	Huf, Hufe	Meerschweinchen	guinea pig

horse	Pferd
kitten	Kätzchen
to lay eggs	Eier legen
to moo	muhen
mouse, mice	Maus, Mäuse
to neigh	wiehern
oats	Hafer
pet	Haustier
pig	Schwein
piglet	Ferkel
puppy	Welpe
rabbit	Kaninchen
rat	Ratte
sheep, sheep	Schaf, Schafe
to squeak	quieken
squirrel	Eichhörnchen
straw	Stroh
tail	Schwanz
tortoise	Landschildkröte
turtle	Wasserschildkröte
to walk the dog/	mit dem Hund
to take the dog for	Gassi gehen
a walk	
wing	Flügel

Milch geben	to give milk
mit dem Hund	to walk the dog/
Gassi gehen	to take the dog for
	a walk
muhen	to moo
Pferd	horse
quaken	to croak
quieken	to squeak
Ratte	rat
Schaf, Schafe	sheep, sheep
Schmetterling	butterfly
Schnabel	beak
Schwanz	tail
Schwein	pig
Stroh	straw
Tier	animal
Tierheim	animal centre
Vogel	bird
Wasserschildkröte	turtle
Wellensittich	budgie
Welpe	puppy
wiehern	to neigh
Ziege	goat
zwitschern	to chirp

Have you got a pet?

Yes, I've got a cat.

What does your dog look like?

My dog is black and white. It has got a long tail.

station

train

plane

taxi

zebra crossing

scooter

underground

bike

Buckingham Palace

traffic light

skateboard

inline skates

guard

Tickets, please.

VISIT LONDON!

double-decker bus

Read and listen.

Listen to the song and sing:

The wheels on the bus

Find the guards.

Where is the ferry?

Tap the underground station.

helicopter

Tower Bridge

WELCOME TO LONDON

Taxi!

ship

lorry

street

London Eye

car

Big Ben

bus driver

schoolbus

ferry

River Thames

? Find the double-decker bus.

? Who is riding a bike?

? Tap Tower Bridge.

? Find the London Eye.

? Where is Buckingham Palace?

? Find Sally.

bike	Fahrrad	Ampel	traffic light
bus driver	Busfahrer/in	aussteigen	to get off
to buy a ticket	eine Fahrkarte kaufen	Auto	car
car	Auto	Bahnhof, Haltestelle	station
to change	umsteigen	Bahnsteig	platform
delayed	verspätet	Busfahrer/in	bus driver
double-decker bus	Doppeldeckerbus	Doppeldeckerbus	double-decker bus
to drive	fahren	einsteigen	to get on
ferry	Fähre	Fähre	ferry
to get off	aussteigen	fahren	to drive
to get on	einsteigen	(Fahrrad) fahren	to ride (a bike)
Great Britain	Großbritannien	Fahrkarte	ticket
guard	Wache	eine Fahrkarte kaufen	to buy a ticket
helicopter	Hubschrauber		
inline skates	Inlineskates	Fahrplan	timetable
king	König	Fahrrad	bike
left-hand traffic	Linksverkehr	Flugzeug	plane
lorry	LKW	Fußgänger	pedestrian
map	Karte	gehen, laufen	to walk
on time	pünktlich	Großbritannien	Great Britain
palace	Schloss	Hubschrauber	helicopter
pedestrian	Fußgänger	Inlineskates	inline skates
plane	Flugzeug	Karte	map
platform	Bahnsteig	König	king
prince	Prinz	Königin	queen
princess	Prinzessin	Königliche Familie	Royal Family
queen	Königin	langsam	slow
to ride (a bike)	(Fahrrad) fahren	Linksverkehr	left-hand traffic
right-hand traffic	Rechtsverkehr	LKW	lorry
River Thames	Themse	(den Bus) nehmen	to take (the bus)
road, street	Straße	Prinz	prince
Royal Family	Königliche Familie	Prinzessin	princess
schoolbus	Schulbus	pünktlich	on time
scooter	Roller, Vespa	Rechtsverkehr	right-hand traffic
ship	Schiff	Roller, Vespa	scooter
skateboard	Skateboard	Schiff	ship

slow	langsam	Schloss	palace
station	Bahnhof,	Schulbus	schoolbus
	Haltestelle	Skateboard	skateboard
to take (the bus)	(den Bus) nehmen	Straße	road, street
taxi	Taxi	Straßenbahn	tram
ticket	Fahrkarte	Taxi	taxi
timetable	Fahrplan	Themse	River Thames
traffic jam	Verkehrsstau	Transport	transport
traffic light	Ampel	U-Bahn	underground
train	Zug	umsteigen	to change
tram	Straßenbahn	Verkehrsstau	traffic jam
transport	Transport	verspätet	delayed
underground	U-Bahn	Wache	guard
to walk	gehen, laufen	Zebrastreifen	zebra crossing
zebra crossing	Zebrastreifen	Zug	train

Wie kann ich von … nach … gelangen?   How can I get from … to …?

Entschuldigen Sie, wie komme ich nach …?   Excuse me, how can I get to …?

Sie können den/die … nehmen.   You can take the …

Gehen Sie geradeaus.   Go straight on.

Biegen Sie links ab.   Turn left.

Biegen Sie rechts ab.   Turn right.

Können Sie mir helfen?   Can you help me, please?

Ich habe mich verlaufen.   I'm lost.

Ich kann den Weg nicht finden.   I can't find my way.

moon

stc

cobweb

owl

spider

pumpkin

skeleton

Read and listen.

Listen to the rhymes:

♫ Ghost rhyme

♫ Tongue twister

Find the clock.

Where is the mummy?

Tap the skeleton.

Find the vampire.

? Find the three owls sitting together.

? Tap the flying owl.

? Find the cat.

? Find Sally.

blood	Blut	an der Tür klingeln	to ring the doorbell
bonfire, campfire	Lagerfeuer	Angst haben	to be frightened,
broom	Besen		to be scared
cat	Katze	ausgehen zum …	to go out for …
cobweb, spider's web	Spinnennetz	Besen	broom
		Blut	blood
costume	Kostüm	dunkel	dark
dark	dunkel	Eule	owl
to dress up	sich verkleiden	fliegen	to fly
to fly	fliegen	Flügel	wing
to be frightened, to be scared	Angst haben	Geist, Gespenst	ghost
		gruselig	scary
ghost	Geist, Gespenst	heute Abend	tonight
to go out for …	ausgehen zum …	Hexe, Hexen	witch, witches
hat	Hut	Hut	hat
to haunt	spuken	jagen	to hunt
haunted castle	Spukschloss	Katze	cat
to hide	verstecken	klopfen	to knock
to hunt	jagen	Kostüm	costume
jack-o'-lantern	Kürbislaterne	Kürbis	pumpkin
to knock	klopfen	Kürbislaterne	jack-o'-lantern
mask	Maske	Lagerfeuer	bonfire, campfire
midnight	Mitternacht	Maske	mask
monster	Monster	Mitternacht	midnight
moon	Mond	Mond	moon

Why are you so sad?

I haven't got a Halloween costume.

Trick or treat! Give me something sweet to eat.

mummy	Mumie	Monster	monster
night	Nacht	Mumie	mummy
owl	Eule	Nacht	night
to play a trick	Streich spielen	schütteln	to shake
pumpkin	Kürbis	Skelett	skeleton
to ring the doorbell	an der Tür klingeln	Spinne	spider
scary	gruselig	Spinnennetz	cobweb, spider's web
to shake	schütteln		
skeleton	Skelett	spuken	to haunt
spider	Spinne	Spukschloss	haunted castle
star	Stern	Stern	star
sweets	Süßigkeiten	Streich spielen	to play a trick
tonight	heute Abend	Süßes oder Saures!	Trick or treat!
Trick or treat!	Süßes oder Saures!	Süßigkeiten	sweets
vampire	Vampir	Vampir	vampire
wing	Flügel	sich verkleiden	to dress up
witch, witches	Hexe, Hexen	verstecken	to hide

Was für eine tolle Verkleidung! What a great costume!

Ich mag deine Verkleidung. I like your costume.

Lass uns heute Abend zu Halloween um die Häuser ziehen. Let's go out for Halloween tonight.

Lass uns an der Tür klopfen. Let's knock on the door.

Ich habe Angst. I'm scared/frightened.

Was für eine dunkle Nacht! What a dark night!

Europe

elk

present

bell

chimney

snowman

gingerbread

mistletoe

fireplace

Christmas market

candle

We wish you a Merry Christmas!

Christmas carol

Christmas tree

Read and listen.

Listen to the rhymes:

🎵 A chubby little snowman

🎵 Here comes Santa

Listen to the Christmas songs and sing:

🎵 I hear them

🎵 We wish you a Merry Christmas

🎵 Jingle bells

66

Father Christmas

sleigh

reindeer

angel

wish list

Australia

Merry Christmas!

Merry Christmas

Christmas baubles

? Find the snowman.

? Who pulls the sleigh?

? Tap the red present.

? Where is the wish list?

? Tap the bell.

? Where are the stockings?

? Find Sally.

angel	Engel	auspacken	to unwrap
bell	Glocke	Band	ribbon
Boxing Day	Zweiter Weihnachtstag	(einen Schnee-mann) bauen	to build (a snowman)
to build (a snowman)	(einen Schnee-mann) bauen	(ein Geschenk) bekommen	to get (a present)
candle	Kerze	Christkind	Christ Child
chimney	Schornstein	dekorieren	to decorate
Christ Child	Christkind	dekoriert	decorated
Christmas baubles	Weihnachtsbaum-kugeln	Elch	elk
		Engel	angel
Christmas card	Weihnachtskarte	Erster Weihnachtstag	Christmas Day
Christmas carol	Weihnachtslied		
Christmas cracker	Weihnachts-knallbonbon	Geschenk	present
		Geschenkpapier	wrapping paper
Christmas Day	Erster Weihnachtstag	Glocke	bell
		Heiligabend	Christmas Eve
Christmas dinner	Weihnachtsessen	Heilige Nacht	holy night
Christmas Eve	Heiligabend	Honigkuchen	gingerbread
Christmas holidays	Weihnachtsferien	(offener) Kamin	fireplace
Christmas market	Weihnachtsmarkt	Keks	cookie
Christmas tree	Weihnachtsbaum	Kerze	candle
chubby	pummelig	Klingglöckchen	jingle bells
cookie	Keks	Krippe	manger
to decorate	dekorieren	Minzpastete	mince pie
decorated	dekoriert	Mistel(zweig)	mistletoe
elk	Elch	Myrrhe	myrrh
Father Christmas, Santa Claus	Weihnachtsmann	Nussknacker	nutcracker
		Plumpudding	plum pudding
fireplace	(offener) Kamin	pummelig	chubby
to get (a present)	(ein Geschenk) bekommen	Rentier, Rentiere	reindeer, reindeer
		Schlitten	sleigh
gingerbread	Honigkuchen	Schnee	snow
holy night	Heilige Nacht	Schneemann	snowman
incense	Weihrauch	Schornstein	chimney
jingle bells	Klingglöckchen	Stall	stable
manger	Krippe	Stern	star

mince pie	Minzpastete	Strumpf	stocking
mistletoe	Mistel(zweig)	Truthahn	turkey
myrrh	Myrrhe	Weihnachtsbaum	Christmas tree
nutcracker	Nussknacker	Weihnachtsbaum-kugeln	Christmas baubles
plum pudding	Plumpudding		
present	Geschenk	Weihnachtsessen	Christmas dinner
to pull	ziehen	Weihnachtsferien	Christmas holidays
reindeer, reindeer	Rentier, Rentiere	Weihnachtskarte	Christmas card
ribbon	Band	Weihnachts-knallbonbon	Christmas cracker
sleigh	Schlitten		
snow	Schnee	Weihnachtslied	Christmas carol
snowman	Schneemann	Weihnachtsmann	Father Christmas, Santa Claus
stable	Stall		
star	Stern	Weihnachtsmarkt	Christmas market
stocking	Strumpf	Weihrauch	incense
turkey	Truthahn	Wunschzettel	wish list
to unwrap	auspacken	ziehen	to pull
wish list	Wunschzettel	Zweiter Weihnachtstag	Boxing Day
wrapping paper	Geschenkpapier		

Frohe Weihnachten!   Merry Christmas!

Gutes neues Jahr!   Happy New Year!

Ich wünsche dir frohe Weihnachten.   I wish you a Merry Christmas.

Was wünschst du dir zu Weihnachten?   What do you want for Christmas?

Ich wünsche mir … (eine Puppe, …).   I wish for … (a doll, …).

Can you hear Father Christmas and his reindeer?

Yes, I can hear them on the roof.

When do you open your Christmas presents?

On the 25th of December.

house

attic

window

bookshelf

bedroom

bathroom

shower

stairs

bathtub

washbasin

cupboard

lamp

armchair

fridge

table

water-tap

cooker

chair

sofa

kitchen

dining room

cellar

Read and listen.

Listen to the rhyme:

Kangaroo's action rhyme

Tap the ball under the table in the bedroom.

Tap the child behind the sofa in the attic.

bedroom

ed

toilet

living room

door

garage

carpet

garden

? Tap the dogs in front of the fridge.

? Where is the sleeping cat?

? Tap the cat between the chairs in the living room.

? Find Sally.

armchair	Sessel	aufräumen	to tidy up
attic	Speicher	Badewanne	bathtub
bathroom	Badezimmer	Badezimmer	bathroom
bathtub	Badewanne	ein Bad nehmen/	to have a bath
bed	Bett	baden	
bedroom	Schlafzimmer	Bett	bed
bookshelf	Bücherregal	Bücherregal	bookshelf
carpet	Teppich	Dusche	shower
cellar, basement	Keller	duschen	to take a shower
chair	Stuhl	Ecke	corner
to clean	putzen	Esszimmer	dining room
to cook	kochen	Etage	floor
cooker	Herd	Fenster	window
corner	Ecke	Fernseher	TV (television)
corridor	Flur	Flur	corridor
cupboard	Schrank	Garage	garage
desk	Schreibtisch	Garten	garden
dining room	Esszimmer	Handtuch	towel
door	Tür	Haus	house
fence	Zaun	Herd	cooker
flat	Wohnung	Keller	cellar, basement
floor	Etage, Stockwerk	Kleiderschrank	wardrobe
fridge (refrigerator)	Kühlschrank	kochen	to cook
furniture	Möbel	Küche	kitchen
game console	Spielekonsole	Kühlschrank	fridge (refrigerator)
garage	Garage	Lampe	lamp
garden	Garten	Möbel	furniture
to have a bath	ein Bad nehmen/	putzen	to clean
	baden	Regal	shelves
at home	zu Hause	reparieren	to repair
house	Haus	schlafen	to sleep
kitchen	Küche	Schlafzimmer	bedroom
lamp	Lampe	Schrank	cupboard
living room	Wohnzimmer	Schreibtisch	desk
to move	umziehen	Sessel	armchair
to repair	reparieren	Sofa	sofa
room	Zimmer, Raum	Speicher	attic

shelves	Regal		Spielekonsole	game console
shower	Dusche		Stuhl	chair
to sleep	schlafen		Teppich	carpet
sofa	Sofa		Tisch	table
stairs	Treppe		Toilette	toilet
table	Tisch		Treppe	stairs
to take a shower	duschen		Tür	door
to tidy up	aufräumen		umziehen	to move
toilet	Toilette		Waschbecken	washbasin
too big	zu groß		Wasserhahn	water-tap
too old	zu alt		Wohnung	flat
too small	zu klein		Wohnzimmer	living room
towel	Handtuch		Zaun	fence
TV (television)	Fernseher		Zimmer, Raum	room
wardrobe	Kleiderschrank		zu alt	too old
washbasin	Waschbecken		zu groß	too big
water-tap	Wasserhahn		zu Hause	at home
window	Fenster		zu klein	too small

Wo ist …? Where is …?

Ist er/sie im … (Keller, …)? Is he/she in the … (cellar, …)?

Er/Sie ist im … He/She is in …

Ja. Yes, he/she is.

Nein. No, he/she isn't.

Ich bin in/im … I am in the …

Kannst du mir helfen? Can you help me?

Read and listen.

Listen to the song and sing:

Today is Monday

Tap the fruit salad.

Where is the cutlery?

Who has chicken and chips?

That's 3 pounds 50, please.

Enjoy your meal!

knife   fork   spoon

I'd like a cookie, please.

mayonnaise

napkin

ketchup

sausage

pudding

hot dog   mustard

salad

dessert   soup

? Find the child who has a hamburger for lunch.

? Who has a hotdog?

? Find the child who has pizza for lunch.

? Who has a salad?

? Find Sally.

apple	Apfel	Apfel	apple
bean	Bohne	Besteck	cutlery
beef	Rindfleisch	Bohne	bean
bill	Rechnung	Cheeseburger	cheeseburger
cake	Kuchen	Cola	coke
cheese	Käse	Eis(krem)	ice cream
cheeseburger	Cheeseburger	Eistee	iced tea
chicken and chips	Hühnchen mit Pommes frites	Ente	duck
		essen	to eat
chocolate	Schokolade	Fisch	fish
coffee	Kaffee	Fleisch	meat
coke	Cola	Gabel	fork
cookie	Keks	Glas	glass
cup	Tasse	Hamburger	hamburger
to cut	schneiden	Hotdog	hot dog
cutlery	Besteck	Hühnchen mit Pommes frites	chicken and chips
delicious	köstlich		
dessert	Nachtisch	Joghurt	yoghurt
to drink	trinken	Kaffee	coffee
duck	Ente	Kartoffelbrei	mashed potatoes
to eat	essen	Käse	cheese
fish	Fisch	Keks	cookie
fork	Gabel	Kellner(in)	waiter, waitress
fruit salad	Obstsalat	Ketchup	ketchup
glass	Glas	köstlich	delicious
ham	Schinken	Kuchen	cake
hamburger	Hamburger	lecker	tasty
hot dog	Hotdog	Löffel	spoon
ice cream	Eis(krem)	Mayonnaise	mayonnaise
iced tea	Eistee	Messer, Messer	knife, knives
juice	Saft	Mittagessen	lunch
ketchup	Ketchup	Nachtisch	dessert
knife, knives	Messer, Messer	Obstsalat	fruit salad
lunch	Mittagessen	Pizza	pizza
mashed potatoes	Kartoffelbrei	Pudding	pudding
mayonnaise	Mayonnaise	Rechnung	bill
meat	Fleisch	Reis	rice

menu	Speisekarte	Restaurant	restaurant
mustard	Senf	Rindfleisch	beef
napkin	Serviette	Saft	juice
pizza	Pizza	Salat	salad
plate	Teller	Salz	salt
pork	Schweinefleisch	Sandwich	sandwich
pudding	Pudding	Schinken	ham
restaurant	Restaurant	schneiden	to cut
rice	Reis	Schokolade	chocolate
salad	Salat	Schweinefleisch	pork
salt	Salz	Senf	mustard
sandwich	Sandwich	Serviette	napkin
sausage	Würstchen	Spaghetti	spaghetti
soup	Suppe	Speisekarte	menu
spaghetti	Spaghetti	Spinat	spinach
spinach	Spinat	Suppe	soup
spoon	Löffel	Tablett	tray
tasty	lecker	Tasse	cup
tomato sauce	Tomatensoße	Teller	plate
tray	Tablett	Tomatensoße	tomato sauce
vegetarian	vegetarisch	trinken	to drink
waiter, waitress	Kellner(in)	vegetarisch	vegetarian
yoghurt	Joghurt	Würstchen	sausage

Kann ich dir/euch/Ihnen helfen? Can I help you?

Ich hätte gerne … (einen Hamburger, ein Glas Cola, …), bitte. I'd like … (a hamburger, a glass of coke. …), please.

Möchtest du/Möchtet ihr/Möchten Sie etwas zu trinken? Would you like anything to drink?

Kann ich … haben? Can I have …?

Kann ich bitte die Speisekarte/die Rechnung haben? Can I have the menu/bill, please?

Hier, bitte. Here you are.

Das macht … Pfund. That's … pounds.

Danke. Thank you.

Bitte. You're welcome.

Guten Appetit. Enjoy your meal.

playing
football

Goal!

inline skating

skateboarding

reading a book

rope skipping

playing hockey

Read and listen.

Where is the guitar?

Who is playing the trumpet?

Who is skipping rope?

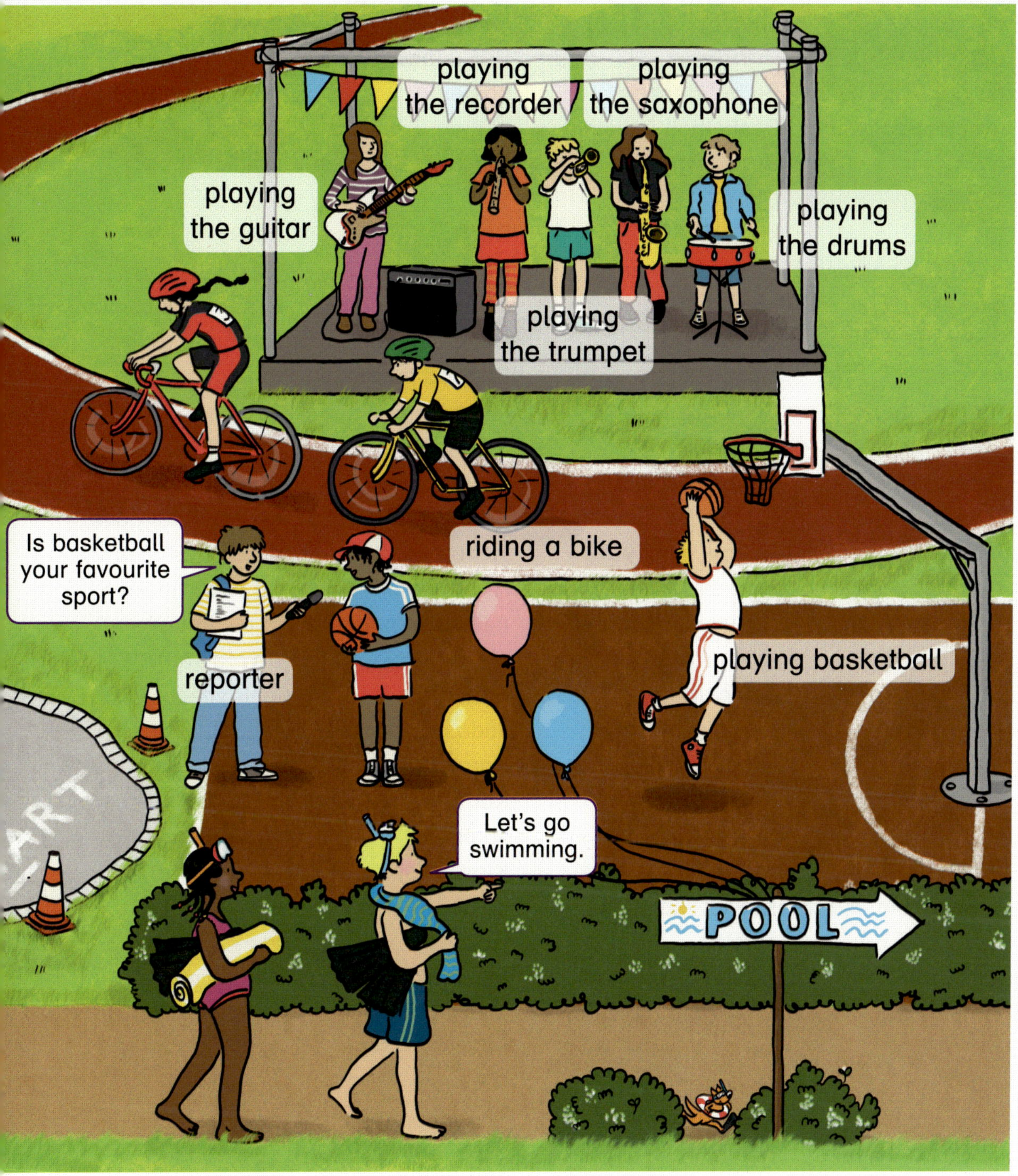

playing
the recorder

playing
the saxophone

playing
the guitar

playing
the drums

playing
the trumpet

Is basketball
your favourite
sport?

riding a bike

reporter

playing basketball

Let's go
swimming.

POOL

? Who is inline skating?

? Who is playing basketball?

? Tap the players in the red team.

? Find Sally.

(to do) arts and crafts	basteln	Ballett (tanzen)	(to do) ballet
(to do) ballet	Ballett (tanzen)	Basketball (spielen)	(to play) basketball
(to play) basketball	Basketball (spielen)	basteln	(to do) arts and crafts
book	Buch	Blockflöte (spielen)	(to play the) recorder
choir	Chor	Buch	book
to climb	klettern	Chor	choir
to collect cards/ stickers	Karten/Sticker sammeln	im Chor singen	to sing in a choir
computer game	Computerspiel	Computerspiel	computer game
to draw	zeichnen	Fahrrad fahren	to ride a bike
(to play the) drums	Schlagzeug (spielen)	fernsehen	to watch TV
(to play) football	Fußball (spielen)	Fußball (spielen)	(to play) football
(to play the) guitar	Gitarre (spielen)	Geige (spielen)	(to play the) violin
hobby, hobbies	Hobby, Hobbys	Gitarre (spielen)	(to play the) guitar
(to play) hockey	Hockey (spielen)	Hobby, Hobbys	hobby, hobbies
to ice-skate	Schlittschuh fahren	Hockey (spielen)	(to play) hockey
to inline skate	Inlineskates fahren	Inlineskates fahren	to inline skate
(to play an) instrument	ein Instrument (spielen)	ein Instrument (spielen)	(to play an) instrument
(to do) judo	Judo (machen)	Judo (machen)	(to do) judo
(to do) karate	Karate (machen)	Karate (machen)	(to do) karate
to listen to music	Musik hören	Karten/Sticker sammeln	to collect cards/ stickers
mountain bike	Mountainbike	Klavier (spielen)	(to play the) piano
(to play the) piano	Klavier (spielen)	klettern	to climb
to play	spielen	lesen	to read
to read	lesen	Mountainbike	mountain bike
(to play the) recorder	Blockflöte (spielen)	Musik hören	to listen to music
reporter	Reporter	reiten	to ride a horse
to ride a bike	Fahrrad fahren	Reporter	reporter
to ride a horse	reiten	Saxophon (spielen)	(to play the) saxophone
(to play the) saxophone	Saxophon (spielen)	Schlagzeug (spielen)	(to play the) drums
to sing	singen	Schlittschuh fahren	to ice-skate
to sing in a choir	im Chor singen	schwimmen	to swim

to skateboard	Skateboard fahren	Seil springen	to skip rope
to skip rope	Seil springen	singen	to sing
to snowboard	snowboarden	Skateboard fahren	to skateboard
sports star	Sportstar	snowboarden	to snowboard
to swim	schwimmen	spielen	to play
(to play) tennis	Tennis (spielen)	Sportstar	sports star
(to play the) trumpet	Trompete (spielen)	Tennis (spielen)	(to play) tennis
(to play the) violin	Geige (spielen)	Trompete (spielen)	(to play the) trumpet
(to play) volleyball	Volleyball (spielen)	Volleyball (spielen)	(to play) volleyball
to watch TV	fernsehen	zeichnen	to draw

Was ist dein Hobby?   What's your hobby?

Mein Hobby ist …   My hobby is …

Kannst du … (Klavier, …) spielen?   Can you play … (the piano, …)?

Kannst du … (Fußball, …) spielen?   Can you play … (football, …)?

Ja./Nein.   Yes, I can./No, I can't.

Welche Sportart/Welches Hobby ist das?   What sport/hobby is it?

Magst du …?   Do you like …?

Ja./Nein.   Yes, I do./No, I don't.

Ich spiele gerne Hockey./Ich singe nicht gerne.   I like playing hockey./ I don't like singing.

Ich würde gerne … (Klavier spielen, reiten, …).   I'd like to … (play the piano, ride a horse, …).

Lass uns … (Tennis, Fußball, …) spielen.   Let's play … (tennis, football, …).

81

My day

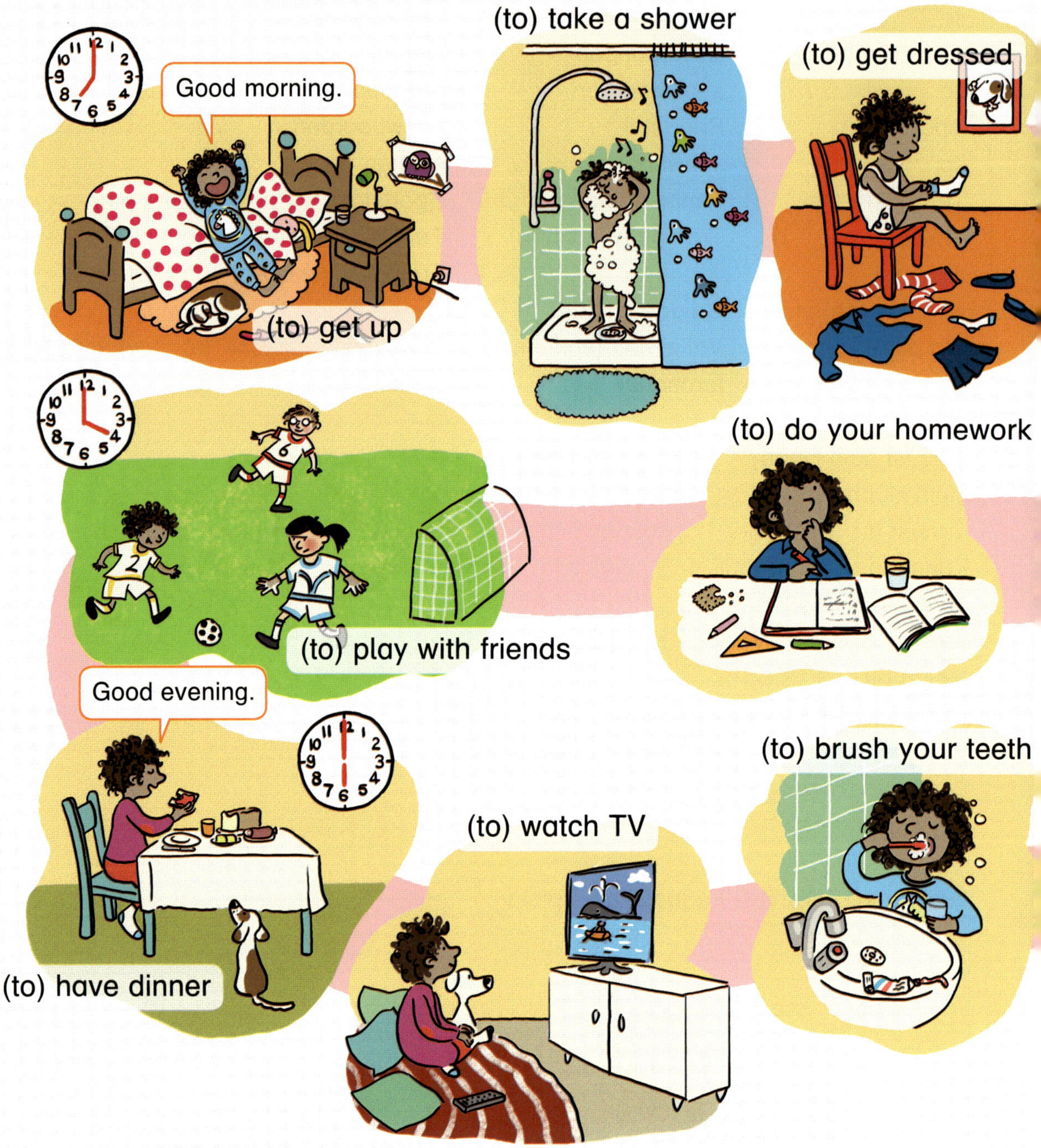
Good morning.
(to) get up
(to) take a shower
(to) get dressed
(to) do your homework
(to) play with friends
Good evening.
(to) have dinner
(to) watch TV
(to) brush your teeth

Read and listen.

Listen to the song and sing:

Through the day

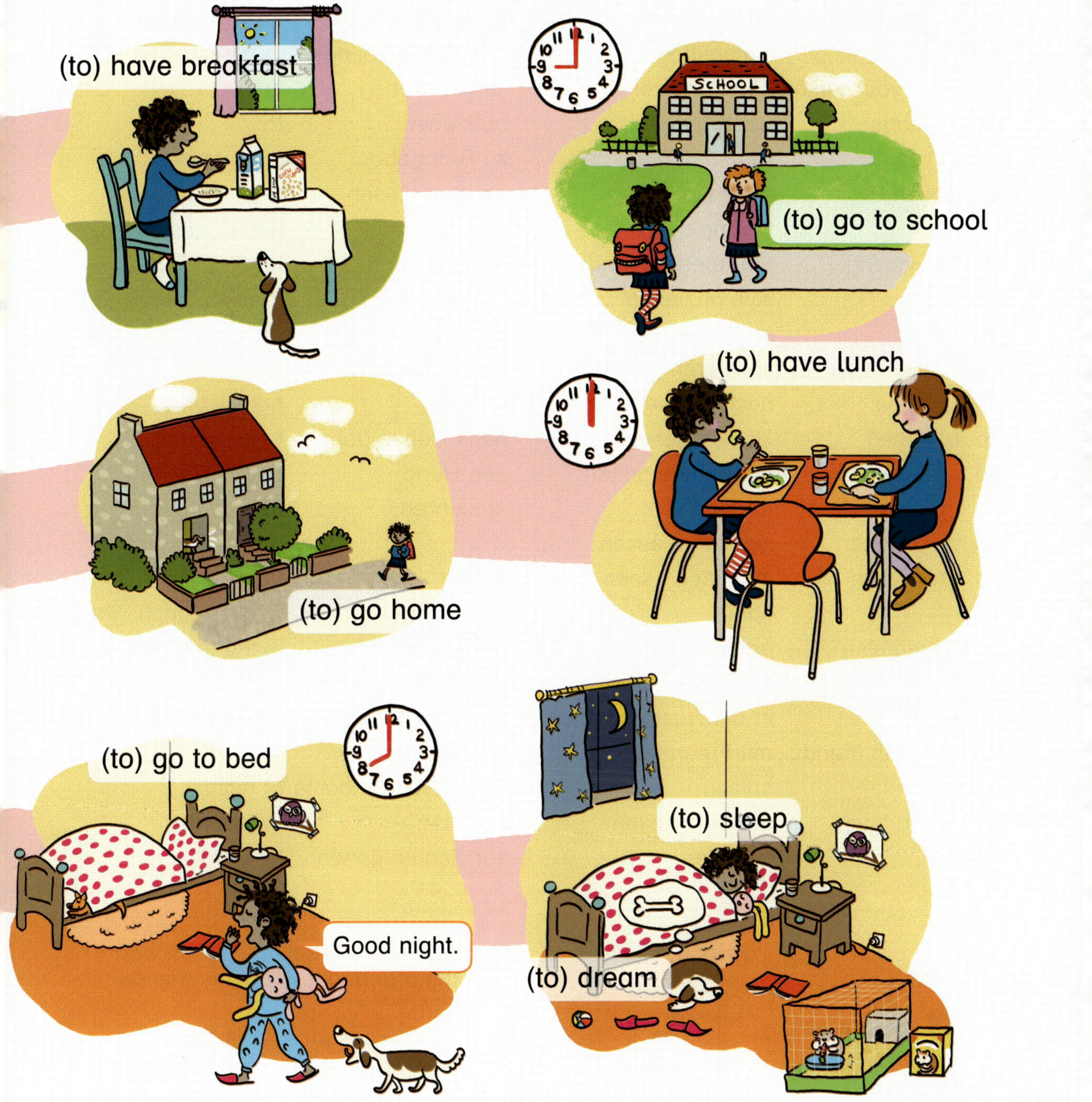
(to) have breakfast
SCHOOL
(to) go to school
(to) have lunch
(to) go home
(to) go to bed
Good night.
(to) sleep
(to) dream

- Who doesn't sleep at night?
- Find the girl doing her homework.
- Find the girl taking a shower.
- It's 4 o'clock. Tap the clock.
- It's 8 o'clock. Tap the clock.
- Find Sally.

in the afternoon	am Nachmittag/ nachmittags	zu Abend essen	to have dinner
to brush your teeth	Zähne putzen	am Abend/abends	in the evening
to do sports	Sport treiben	sich anziehen	to get dressed
to do your homework	Hausaufgaben machen	aufstehen	to get up
to dream	träumen	zu Bett gehen	to go to bed
in the evening	am Abend/abends	ein Buch lesen	to read a book
to get dressed	sich anziehen	duschen	to take a shower
to get up	aufstehen	fernsehen	to watch TV
to go for a walk	spazieren gehen	frühstücken	to have breakfast
to go home	nach Hause gehen	Hände waschen	to wash your hands
to go to bed	zu Bett gehen	Hausaufgaben machen	to do your homework
to go to school	zur Schule gehen	nach Hause gehen	to go home
to have breakfast	frühstücken	den Hund ausführen	to walk the dog/ to take the dog for a walk
to have dinner	zu Abend essen		
to have lunch	zu Mittag essen	lernen	to study
late	spät	zu Mittag essen	to have lunch
in the morning	am Morgen/ morgens	am Morgen/ morgens	in the morning
at night	in der Nacht/nachts	am Nachmittag/ nachmittags	in the afternoon
to play with friends	mit Freunden spielen	in der Nacht/nachts	at night
to read a book	ein Buch lesen	schlafen	to sleep
to sleep	schlafen	zur Schule gehen	to go to school

to study	lernen	spät	late
to take a shower	duschen	spazieren gehen	to go for a walk
to walk the dog/ to take the dog for a walk	den Hund ausführen	mit Freunden spielen	to play with friends
		Sport treiben	to do sports
to wash your hands	Hände waschen	träumen	to dream
to watch TV	fernsehen	Zähne putzen	to brush your teeth

Guten Morgen.   Good morning.

Guten Tag. *(ab 12 Uhr)*   Good afternoon.

Gute Nacht.   Good night.

Guten Abend.   Good evening.

Schlaf gut.   Sleep well.

Entschuldigung, dass ich zu spät bin.   Sorry, I'm late.

Die Schule ist aus.   School is out.

Ich putze meine Zähne.   I brush my teeth.

Ich mache meine Hausaufgaben.   I do my homework.

Ich wasche meine Hände.   I wash my hands.

Wie viel Uhr ist es?   What time is it?

Es ist halb fünf.   It's half past 4.

Es ist Viertel vor fünf.   It's quarter to 5.

Es ist fünf Uhr.   It's 5 o'clock.

Es ist Viertel nach fünf.   It's quarter past 5.

Read and listen.

Listen to the song and sing:

Ten green bottles

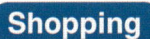

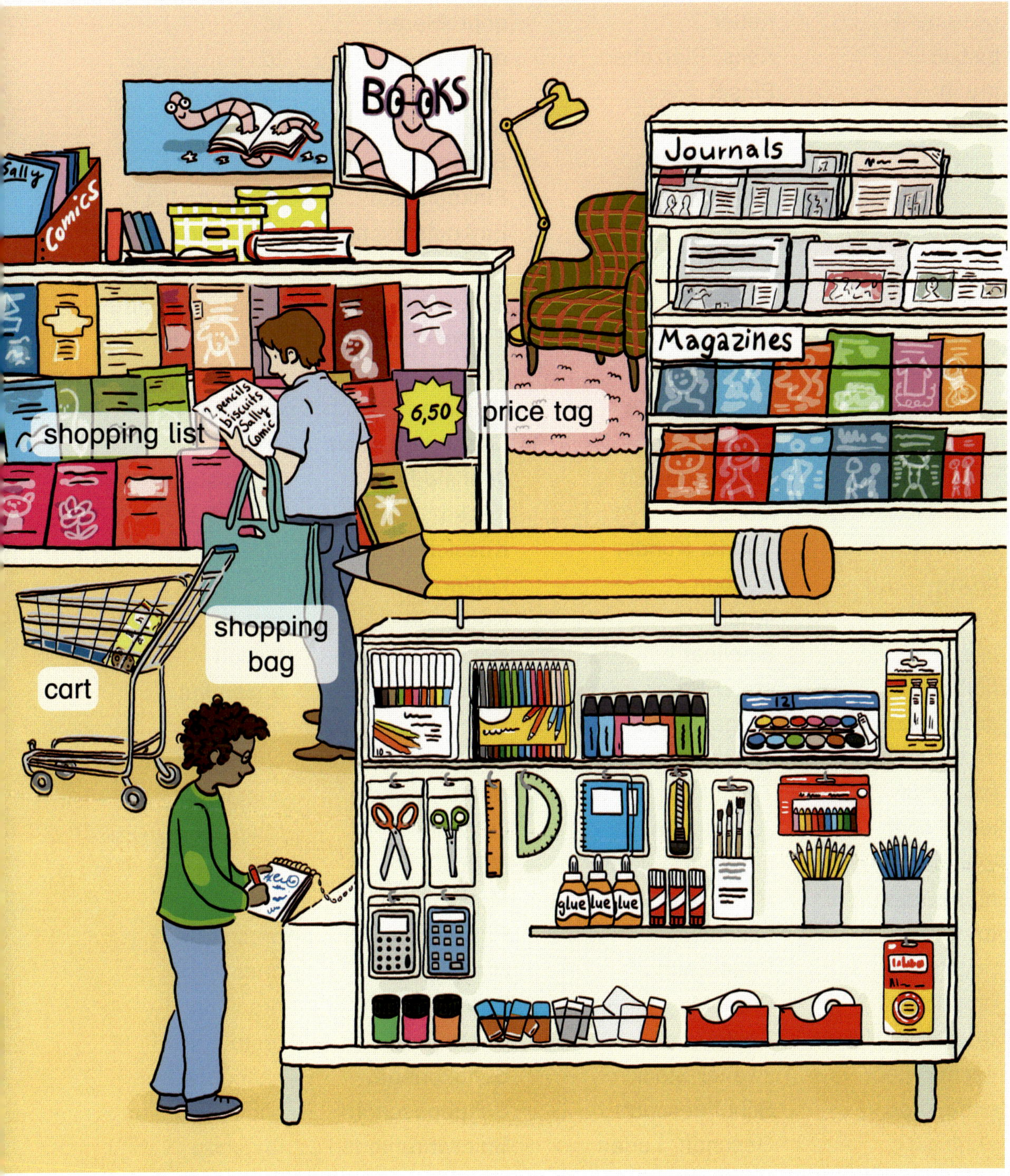
BOOKS
Sally
Comics
Journals
Magazines
2 pencils
biscuits
Sally Comic
6,50
price tag
shopping list
shopping bag
cart
glue
glue
glue

¿ Where is the shopping list?

¿ What is 6 pounds 50 pence?

¿ Who is eating sweets?

¿ Find Sally.

basement	Keller	anprobieren	to try on
biscuit	Keks, Plätzchen	aussuchen	to choose
brush	Pinsel	bezahlen	to pay
to buy	kaufen	billig	cheap
candy	Süßigkeit	Bonbon	drop
cart	Einkaufswagen	Einkaufsliste	shopping list
cash desk	Kasse	Einkaufstasche	shopping bag
cashier	Kassierer(in)	Einkaufswagen	cart
to change	wechseln	Einkaufszentrum	shopping centre
cheap	billig	Erdgeschoss	ground floor
chocolate bar	Schokoriegel	erster Stock	first floor
to choose	aussuchen	Fineliner	fineliner, pen
cinema	Kino	Geschäft, Laden	shop
clothes shop	Kleiderladen	Jeansladen	jeans shop
coin	Münze	Kasse	cash desk
customer	Kunde, Kundin	Kassierer(in)	cashier
drop	Bonbon	kaufen	to buy
expensive	teuer	Kaufhaus	store
fineliner, pen	Fineliner	Keks, Plätzchen	biscuit
first floor	erster Stock	Keller	basement
ground floor	Erdgeschoss	Kino	cinema
ink cartridge	Tintenpatrone	Kleiderladen	clothes shop
ink eraser	Tintenkiller	Kunde, Kundin	customer
jeans shop	Jeansladen	Lutscher	lollipop
lollipop	Lutscher	Münze	coin
music shop	Musikgeschäft	Musikgeschäft	music shop
to pay	bezahlen	Pinsel	brush
price tag	Preisschild	Preisschild	price tag
products	Produkte	Produkte	products
restaurant	Restaurant	Restaurant	restaurant
second floor	zweiter Stock	Schokoriegel	chocolate bar
shoe shop	Schuhgeschäft	Schuhgeschäft	shoe shop
shop	Geschäft, Laden	Spielwarenladen	toy shop
shop assistant	Verkäufer(in)	Sportgeschäft	sports shop
shopping bag	Einkaufstasche	Supermarkt	supermarket
shopping centre	Einkaufszentrum	Süßigkeit	candy
shopping list	Einkaufsliste	Süßigkeiten	sweets

sports shop	Sportgeschäft	Süßwarenladen	sweet shop
store	Kaufhaus	teuer	expensive
supermarket	Supermarkt	Tintenkiller	ink eraser
sweet shop	Süßwarenladen	Tintenpatrone	ink cartridge
sweets	Süßigkeiten	Verkäufer(in)	shop assistant
too big	zu groß	wechseln	to change
too small	zu klein	zu groß	too big
toy shop	Spielwarenladen	zu klein	too small
to try on	anprobieren	zweiter Stock	second floor

Kann ich dir/euch/Ihnen helfen? Can I help you?

Können Sie/kannst du mir helfen? Can you help me?

Ja, ich suche ein/e … Yes, I'm looking for a …

Probiere/Probieren Sie es an. Try it on.

Gefällt es dir/euch/Ihnen? Do you like it?

Ja/Nein. Yes, I do./No, I don't.

Es ist zu groß/klein. It's too big/small.

Mir gefällt … (die Farbe, …) nicht. I don't like … (the colour, …).

Wie viel kostet es? How much is it?

Es kostet … Pfund./Das macht … Pfund. It's … pounds./That's … pounds.

Bitte sehr. Here you are.

Wo kann ich ein/e … kaufen? Where can I buy a …?

Du kannst es in einem (Sport-, …) Geschäft kaufen. You can buy it in a (sports, …) shop.

Hast du … auf deiner Einkaufsliste? Have you got … on your shopping list?

polar bear

wolf

griz:

zookeeper

tiger

penguin

seal

dolphin

hippo

crocodile

koala

parrot

kangaroo

ZOO

Read and listen.

Listen to the song and sing:

Walking through the jungle

Listen to the rhyme:

Five little monkeys

Guess my animal. Tap it.

It's very big. It's grey. It has got a trunk.

It can climb. It's very funny. It's brown.

90

monkey

rhino

snake

gorilla

elephant

lion

flamingo

camel

zebra

giraffe

tortoise

(?) My animal has no legs. It's very long. It can be dangerous.

(?) It's very slow. It's not dangerous. It can get very old.

(?) It's big and very dangerous. It's the king of the jungle.

(?) Find Sally.

(?) It's black and white. It looks like a horse.

beak	Schnabel	Adler	eagle
bear	Bär	Affe	monkey
big, tall	groß, hoch	Bär	bear
to bite	beißen	beißen	to bite
camel	Kamel	brüllen	to roar
clever	schlau	Delfin	dolphin
to climb	klettern	dick, fett	fat
crocodile	Krokodil	Dschungel	jungle
dangerous	gefährlich	Eisbär	polar bear
to dive	tauchen	Elefant	elephant
dolphin	Delfin	essen, fressen	to eat
eagle	Adler	Fell	fur
to eat	essen, fressen	Flamingo	flamingo
elephant	Elefant	fliegen	to fly
fast	schnell	Flosse	fin
fat	dick, fett	Flügel	wing
fin	Flosse	gefährlich	dangerous
flamingo	Flamingo	Giraffe	giraffe
to fly	fliegen	Gorilla	gorilla
funny	komisch, lustig	Grizzly(-bär)	grizzly (bear)
fur	Fell	groß, hoch	big, tall
giraffe	Giraffe	Hai(-fisch)	shark
gorilla	Gorilla	hoch	tall
grizzly (bear)	Grizzly(-bär)	Kamel	camel
hippo	Nilpferd	Känguru	kangaroo
jungle	Dschungel	klein	small
kangaroo	Känguru	klettern	to climb
koala (bear)	Koala(-bär)	Koala(-bär)	koala (bear)
lion	Löwe	komisch, lustig	funny
long	lang	Krokodil	crocodile
mane	Mähne	lang	long
monkey	Affe	Löwe	lion
parrot	Papagei	Mähne	mane
penguin	Pinguin	Nashorn	rhino
polar bear	Eisbär	Nilpferd	hippo
rhino	Nashorn	Papagei	parrot
to roar	brüllen	Pinguin	penguin

to run	rennen, laufen	rennen, laufen	to run
seal	Robbe, Seehund	Robbe, Seehund	seal
shark	Hai(-fisch)	Rüssel	trunk
small	klein	Schildkröte	tortoise
snake	Schlange	Schlange	snake
strong	stark	schlau	clever
to swim	schwimmen	Schnabel	beak
tail	Schwanz	schnell	fast
tall, big	hoch, groß	Schwanz	tail
tiger	Tiger	schwimmen	to swim
tortoise	Schildkröte	stark	strong
trunk	Rüssel	tauchen	to dive
wing	Flügel	Tierpfleger(in)	zookeeper
wolf	Wolf	Tiger	tiger
zebra	Zebra	Wolf	wolf
zoo	Zoo	Zebra	zebra
zookeeper	Tierpfleger(in)	Zoo	zoo

Errate mein Tier.   Guess my animal.

Es hat … (einen Schwanz, einen Rüssel, …).   It's got … (a tail, a trunk, …).

Es ist … (klein, schlau, lustig, …).   It's … (small, clever, funny, …).

Es kann … (schwimmen, fliegen, klettern, …).   It can … (swim, fly, climb, …).

Welches ist dein Lieblingstier?   What's your favourite animal?

Ich mag … am liebsten.   I like … best.

hospital

waiting room

My back hurts.

patient

doctor

prescription

Read and listen.

Listen to the song and sing:

The Hokey Cokey

Listen. Find the correct person and tap.

I've got a headache.

My arm hurts.

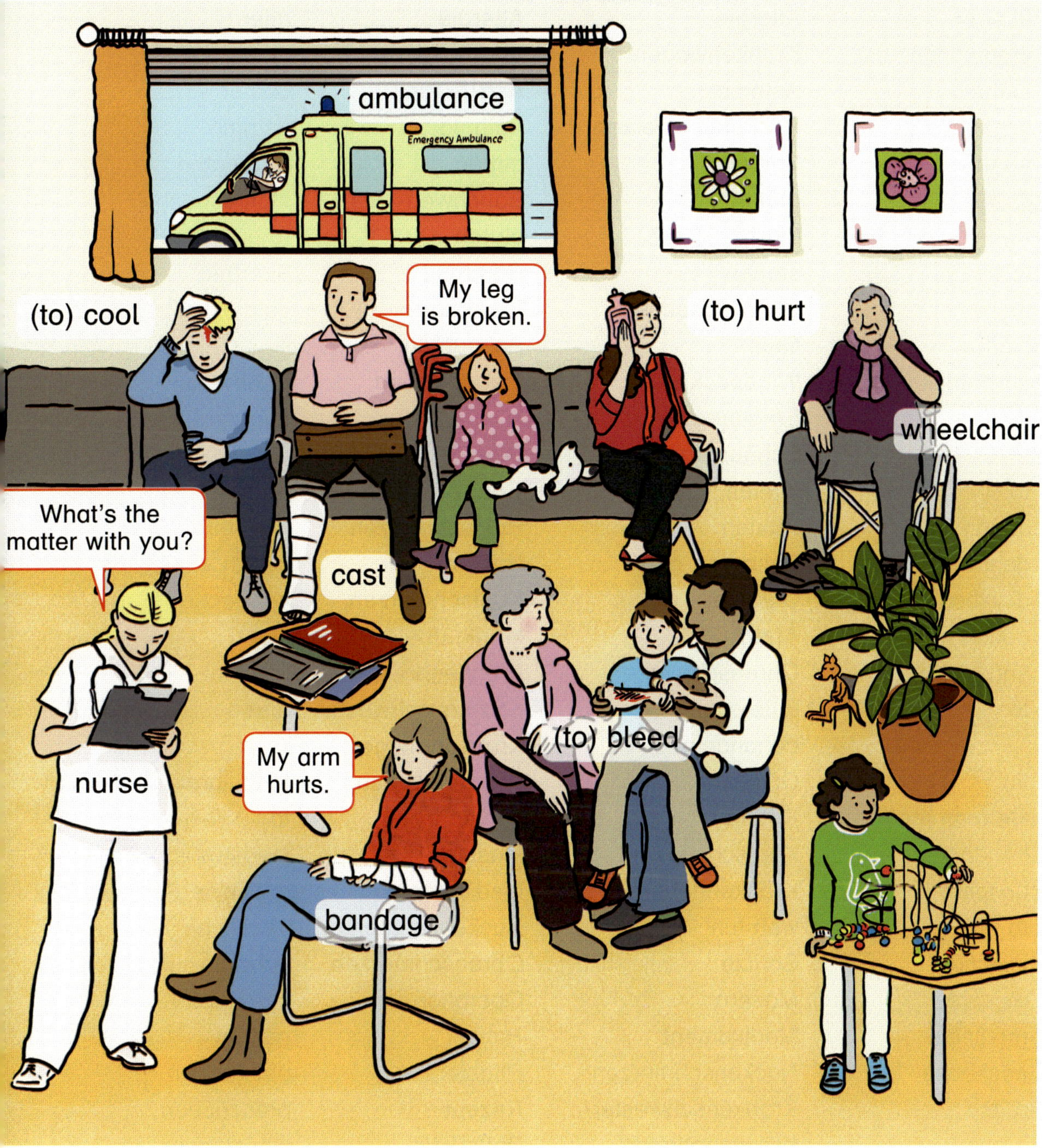
ambulance
Emergency Ambulance
(to) cool
My leg is broken.
(to) hurt
wheelchair
What's the matter with you?
cast
nurse
My arm hurts.
(to) bleed
bandage

- I've got backache.
- My neck hurts.
- I've got earache.
- My leg is broken.
- Where is the doctor?
- Find Sally.

allergy	Allergie	Allergie	allergy
ambulance	Krankenwagen	Apotheke	pharmacy
asthma	Asthma	Arzt/Ärztin	doctor
backache	Rückenschmerzen	Asthma	asthma
bandage	Verband	atmen	to breathe
to bleed	bluten	Bauchweh	stomachache
to breathe	atmen	bluten	to bleed
to bump	stoßen	Durchfall	diarrhea
to burn	sich verbrennen	Erkältung,	cold
cast	Gips	Schnupfen	
chickenpox	Windpocken	Fieber haben	to have a
cold	Erkältung,		temperature
	Schnupfen	Gips	cast
to cool	kühlen	Grippe	flu
cough	Husten	Halsschmerzen	sore throat
dentist	Zahnarzt/-ärztin	Husten	cough
diarrhea	Durchfall	Kopfschmerzen	headache
doctor	Arzt/Ärztin	krank, übel	sick
earache	Ohrenschmerzen	Krankenhaus	hospital
to examine	untersuchen,	Krankenschwester/	nurse
	behandeln	Krankenpfleger	
flu	Grippe	Krankenwagen	ambulance
German measles	Röteln	kühlen	to cool
headache	Kopfschmerzen	Masern	measles
hospital	Krankenhaus	Medikament	medicine
to hurt	weh tun	Nackenschmerzen	neckache
injection	Spritze	Ohrenschmerzen	earache
measles	Masern	Operation	operation
medicine	Medikament	Patient	patient
neckache	Nackenschmerzen	Pflaster	plaster
nurse	Krankenschwester/	Rezept	prescription
	Krankenpfleger	Rollstuhl	wheelchair
operation	Operation	Röteln	German measles
patient	Patient	Rückenschmerzen	backache
pharmacy	Apotheke	Spritze	injection
pill	Tablette	stoßen	to bump
plaster	Pflaster	Tablette	pill

prescription	Rezept	Taschentücher	tissues
sick	krank, übel	Thermometer	thermometer
sore throat	Halsschmerzen	sich übergeben	to vomit
stomachache	Bauchweh	untersuchen, behandeln	to examine
to have a temperature	Fieber haben	Verband	bandage
thermometer	Thermometer	sich verbrennen	to burn
tissues	Taschentücher	Wartezimmer	waiting room
toothache	Zahnschmerzen	weh tun	to hurt
to vomit	sich übergeben	Windpocken	chickenpox
waiting room	Wartezimmer	Wunde	wound
wheelchair	Rollstuhl	Zahnarzt/-ärztin	dentist
wound	Wunde	Zahnschmerzen	toothache

Aua.   Ouch!

Lass uns zum Arzt gehen.   Let's go to the doctor's.

Der Nächste, bitte.   Next, please.

Was fehlt dir/Ihnen?   What's the matter (with you)?

Mir geht es gut.   I'm fine.

Ich bin krank.   I'm sick.

Ich habe …   I've got a/an …

Mein … tut weh.   My … hurts.

Hole ein Pflaster oder einen Verband.   Get a plaster or a bandage.

Kühle es.   Cool it.

Rufe 112 an.   Call 112.

What's the matter with you?

I'm sick. I've got a headache.

You've got a high temperature. Let's go to the doctor's.

I feel sick.

millionaire

singer

pilot

(to) work in the garden

football player

shop assistant

teacher

(to) do my homework

(to) help in the kitchen

(to) walk the dog

Read and listen.

Listen to the rhyme:

Hey, my name is Joe

Who is working in the garden?

Find the policemen.

Who is doing homework in the living room?

policeman

(to) tidy
my room

vet

(to) feed
the cat

HAIR SALON

Bakery

Bread

? Find the bakery.

? Tap the hairdresser.

? Who is walking the dog?

? Tap the vet.

? Find Sally.

99

actor, actress	Schauspieler(in)	arbeiten	to work
architect	Architekt(in)	arbeitslos	jobless
artist	Künstler(in)	Architekt(in)	architect
bank clerk	Bankangestellte(r)	Arzt/Ärztin	(medical) doctor
dentist	Zahnarzt/-ärztin	Bankangestellte(r)	bank clerk
designer	Designer(in)	Bauer/Bäuerin	farmer
to do my homework	meine Hausaufgaben machen	Beruf, Aufgabe	job
		Designer(in)	designer
		Elektriker(in)	electrician
to earn money	Geld verdienen	Feuerwehrmann/ -frau	firefighter
electrician	Elektriker(in)		
engineer	Ingenieur(in)	Flugbegleiter(in)	flight attendant
farmer	Bauer/Bäuerin	Footballspieler(in)	football player
to feed (the cat, …)	(die Katze, …) füttern	(die Katze, …) füttern	to feed (the cat, …)
firefighter	Feuerwehrmann/ -frau	Friseur(in)	hairdresser
		Geld verdienen	to earn money
flight attendant	Flugbegleiter(in)	den Hund ausführen	to walk the dog
football player	Footballspieler(in)		
hairdresser	Friseur(in)	in der Küche/im Garten/im Haus helfen	to help in the kitchen/garden/ house
to help in the kitchen/garden/ house	in der Küche/im Garten/im Haus helfen		
		Ingenieur(in)	engineer
job	Beruf, Aufgabe	Journalist(in)	journalist
jobless	arbeitslos	Kindergärtner(in)	nursery teacher
journalist	Journalist(in)	Klempner(in)	plumber
judge	Richter(in)	Krankenschwester/ Krankenpfleger	nurse
lawyer	Rechtsanwalt/ -anwältin		
		Künstler(in)	artist
to make my bed	mein Bett machen	Lehrer(in)	teacher
manager	Manager(in)	Maler(in)	painter
mechanic	Mechaniker(in)	Manager(in)	manager
(medical) doctor	Arzt/Ärztin	Mechaniker(in)	mechanic
millionaire	Millionär(in)	mein Bett machen	to make my bed
musician	Musiker(in)	meine Hausaufgaben machen	to do my homework
nurse	Krankenschwester/ Krankenpfleger		

nursery teacher	Kindergärtner(in)	mein Zimmer aufräumen	to tidy my room
painter	Maler(in)		
pilot	Pilot(in)	Millionär(in)	millionaire
plumber	Klempner(in)	Musiker(in)	musician
policeman/-woman	Polizist(in)	Pilot(in)	pilot
programmer	Programmierer(in)	Polizist(in)	policeman/-woman
shop assistant	Verkäufer(in)	Programmierer(in)	programmer
singer	Sänger(in)	Rechtsanwalt/ -anwältin	lawyer
teacher	Lehrer(in)		
technician	Techniker(in)	Richter(in)	judge
to tidy my room	mein Zimmer aufräumen	Sänger(in)	singer
		Schauspieler(in)	actor/actress
vet	Tierarzt/-ärztin	Techniker(in)	technician
to walk the dog	den Hund ausführen	Tierarzt/-ärztin	vet
		Verkäufer(in)	shop assistant
to work	arbeiten	Zahnarzt/-ärztin	dentist

Was möchtest du werden?   What do you want to be?

Ich möchte … werden.   I want to be a …

Was machst du beruflich?   What's your job?

Ich bin …   I'm a …

Welche Aufgabe hast du im Haushalt/in deiner Gruppe?   What's your job around the house/in your group?

Welche Aufgaben hast du zu Hause?   What are your jobs at home?

Ich muss … (in der Küche helfen, …).   I have to … (help in the kitchen, …).

What's your job?

I'm a hairdresser.

What do you want to be?

I want to be a pilot.

Read and listen.

Listen to the song and sing:

We all live in the same world

Terminal 1		Time	Gate
✈ Flight Arrivals	Paris/France	10:45	A 3
	Berlin/Germany	10:50	A 21
	London/Great Britain	11:05	A 5
	Madrid/Spain	12:00	A 9
	Istanbul/Turkey	12:30	B 10
	New York/USA	12:45	B 12
	Tokyo/Japan	13:00	B 8

plane

Afghanistan

Australia   Russia   Greece   Iraq

Ireland

Where are you from?

I'm from Canada.

Check-in

choose your language

? Who is from Canada?

? Tap the German flag.

? Which flight arrives at 12:30? Tap.

? Tap the British flag.

? Tap the Turkish flag.

? Find Sally.

Africa	Afrika	Afrika	Africa
airport	Flughafen	Amerika	America
America	Amerika	Asien	Asia
Asia	Asien	Australien	Australia
Australia	Australien	Europa	Europe
continent	Kontinent	Flüchtling	refugee
country	Land	Flughafen	airport
Europe	Europa	Flugzeug	plane
language	Sprache	Kontinent	continent
to live	leben	Land	country
to meet	treffen	leben	to live
nationality	Nationalität	Nationalität	nationality
passport	(Reise-)Pass	(Reise-)Pass	passport
plane	Flugzeug	reisen	to travel
refugee	Flüchtling	Sprache	language
to speak	sprechen	sprechen	to speak
to travel	reisen	treffen	to meet
to understand	verstehen	verstehen	to understand
world	Welt	Welt	world

Woher kommst du?   Where are you from?

Ich komme aus …   I'm from …

Kommst du aus …?   Are you from …?

Sprichst du …?   Can you speak …?/Do you speak …?

Welche Sprachen sprichst du?   Which languages can you speak?

Ich spreche …   I can speak …

Was ist deine Nationalität/Staatsangehörigkeit?   What's your nationality?

Ich bin … (Afrikaner, …).   I'm … (African, …).

Land	country	Sprache	language
Afghanistan	Afghanistan	Paschtunisch	Pashto
Ägypten	Egypt	Arabisch	Arabic
Albanien	Albania	Albanisch	Albanian
Australien	Australia	Englisch	English
Belgien	Belgium	Französisch	French
Brasilien	Brazil	Portugiesisch	Portuguese
China	China	Chinesisch	Chinese

Land	country	Sprache	language
Dänemark	Denmark	Dänisch	Danish
Deutschland	Germany	Deutsch	German
Estland	Estonia	Estnisch	Estonian
Finnland	Finland	Finnisch	Finnish
Frankreich	France	Französisch	French
Georgien	Georgia	Georgisch	Georgian
Griechenland	Greece	Griechisch	Greek
Großbritannien	Great Britain	Englisch	English
Irak	Iraq	Arabisch	Arabic
Iran	Iran	Persisch	Persian
Irland	Ireland	Englisch	English
Israel	Israel	Hebräisch	Hebrew
Italien	Italy	Italienisch	Italian
Japan	Japan	Japanisch	Japanese
Kanada	Canada	Englisch	English
Kroatien	Croatia	Kroatisch	Croatian
Lettland	Latvia	Lettisch	Latvian
Litauen	Lithuania	Litauisch	Lithuanian
Neuseeland	New Zealand	Englisch	English
Niederlande	Netherlands	Holländisch	Dutch
Norwegen	Norway	Norwegisch	Norwegian
Österreich	Austria	Deutsch	German
Polen	Poland	Polnisch	Polish
Portugal	Portugal	Portugiesisch	Portuguese
Rumänien	Romania	Rumänisch	Romanian
Russland	Russia	Russisch	Russian
Schweiz	Switzerland	Deutsch	German
Spanien	Spain	Spanisch	Spanish
Syrien	Syria	Arabisch	Arabic
Tschechische Republik	Czech Republic	Tschechisch	Czech
Tschetschenien	Chechenia	Tschetschenisch	Chechen
Türkei	Turkey	Türkisch	Turkish
Ungarn	Hungary	Ungarisch	Hungarian
USA	USA	Englisch	English
Weißrussland	Belarus	Russisch	Russian

Anhang

Verbs

to climb

to love

to calculate

to buy (a ticket)

to drink

to clean

to count

to eat

to help

to listen to (music)

to dance

to draw

to play

to feed

to sleep

to walk

to put on

to take off

to write

to wash

to swim

to run

to sing

to tidy up

to read

to watch

to speak

to wait

stupid   clever

Sally is stupid.
Sam is clever.

slow   fast

The tortoise is slow.
The zebra is fast.

long   short

The girl has got long hair.
The boy has got short hair.

sad   happy

Sam is sad.
Sally is happy.

tired   fit

The koala is tired.
The monkey is fit.

hot   cold

The tea is hot.
The lemonade is cold.

cheap   expensive

The car is cheap.
The doll is expensive.

wet   dry

The T-shirt is wet.
The skirt is dry.

loud   quiet

The parrot is loud.
The fish is quiet.

dirty   clean

Sally is dirty.
Sam is clean.

big	small

The elephant is big
The mouse is small.

boring	exciting

Sam's book is boring.
Sally's book is exciting.

old	young

Grandma is old.
The baby is young.

full	hungry

Sally is full.
Sam is hungry.

old	new

Sally's shoes are old.
Sam's shoes are new.

dark	light

The pullover is dark green.
The T-shirt is light green.

fat	thin

The hippo is fat.
The snake is thin.

full	empty

Sally's pouch is full.
Sam's pouch is empty.

tall	little

The giraffe is tall.
The mouse is little.

left	right

Sally turns left.
Sam turns right.

into
in

out of
aus

in
in

on
auf

under
unter

next to
neben

opposite to
gegenüber

down
hinunter

up
hinauf

through
durch

over
über

behind
hinter

in front of
vor

between
zwischen

across
hinüber

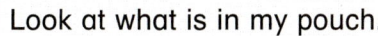

Look at what is in my pouch.

Numbers

1 one	11 eleven	21 twenty-one	
2 two	12 twelve	22 twenty-two	
3 three	13 thirteen	23 twenty-three	
4 four	14 fourteen	24 twenty-four	
5 five	15 fifteen	25 twenty-five	40 forty
6 six	16 sixteen	26 twenty-six	50 fifty
7 seven	17 seventeen	27 twenty-seven	60 sixty
8 eight	18 eighteen	28 twenty-eight	70 seventy
9 nine	19 nineteen	29 twenty-nine	80 eighty
10 ten	20 twenty	30 thirty	90 ninety

a/one hundred	100
a/one thousand	1 000
ten thousand	10 000
a/one hundred thousand	100 000
a/one million	1 000 000
a/one billion	1 000 000 000

first 1st **1.** erste/r

second 2nd **2.** zweite/r

third 3rd **3.** dritte/r

fourth 4th **4.** vierte/r

fifth 5th **5.** fünfte/r

sixth 6th **6.** sechste/r

seventh 7th **7.** siebte/r

eighth 8th **8.** achte/r

ninth 9th **9.** neunte/r

tenth 10th **10.** zehnte/r

to past

o'clock · quarter to · quarter past · half past

eight o'clock

a quarter past eight
(eight fifteen)

half past eight
(eight thirty)

a quarter to nine
(eight forty-five)

ten past eight
(eight ten)

twenty-five past eight
(eight twenty-five)

twenty to nine
(eight forty)

four to nine
(eight fifty-six)

a.m. (ante meridiem)
vor 12 Uhr mittags

noon

in the morning

p.m. (post meridiem)
nach 12 Uhr mittags

in the afternoon

in the evening

at night

What time is it?

It's 9 o'clock.

115

Hilfsverben

Kurzformen und Verneinungen

Hilfsverben (wie z. B. can und have) und ihre Verneinungen kann man im Englischen auch abkürzen, indem man Buchstaben durch ein Apostroph (') ersetzt.

I can	Ich kann
I do	Ich tue/mache
I have – I've	Ich habe
I am – I'm	Ich bin
You are – You're	Du bist
It is – It's	Es ist
I would like – I'd like	Ich würde/hätte gern

I cannot – I can't	Ich kann nicht
I do not – I don't	Ich tue/mache nicht
I have not – I haven't	Ich habe nicht
I am not – I'm not	Ich bin nicht
You are not – You aren't	Du bist nicht
It is not – It isn't	Es ist nicht
I would not like – I wouldn't like	Ich würde/hätte nicht gern

Verbformen

In der Gegenwart wird bei he/she/it ein **s** an das Verb angehängt.
Bei allen anderen Personalformen (I/you/we/you/they) bleibt das Verb unverändert.

He/she/it – das **s** muss mit:
I swim – **he/she/it** swim**s**
You play – **he/she/it** play**s**

In der Vergangenheit wird an Verben **-ed** angehängt (regelmäßige Verben):
I play – I play**ed**, I jump – I jump**ed**

Hier gibt es bei einigen Verben eine Ausnahme (unregelmäßige Verben):
I sing – I sang, I go – I went, …

Plural (Mehrzahl)

Im Englischen wird der Plural meistens mit **s** gebildet (regelmäßiger Plural):
one knee – two knee**s**, one apple – two apple**s**, one dog – two dog**s**

Es gibt Ausnahmen, die man sich merken muss (unregelmäßiger Plural):
one foot – two feet, one fish – two fish, one mouse – two mice,
one child – two children, one knife – two knives, one baby – two babies,
one tomato – two tomatoes, one glass – two glasses, …

Artikel

Die bestimmten Artikel **der, die, das** heißen im Englischen **the**.
the dog, **the** banana, **the** pencil
Die unbestimmten Artikel **ein, eine** heißen im Englischen **a**.
a dog, **a** banana, **a** pencil

Achtung: Hörst du am Anfang eines Wortes einen Vokal, wird das **a** zu **an**:
an apple, **an** elephant, …

Pronomen

Nominativ	Genitiv	Dativ	Akkusativ
Wer geht zur Schule? Who goes to school?	Wessen Ball ist es? Whose ball is it?	Wem gehört das Bett? Whose bed is it?	Wen mag Sally? Whom does Sally like?
I go to school.	This is **my** ball.	The bed is **mine**.	Sally likes **me**.
You go to school.	This is **your** ball.	The bed is **yours**.	Sally likes **you**.
He/She goes to school.	This is **his/her** ball.	The bed is **his/hers**.	Sally likes **him/her**.
We go to school.	This is **our** ball.	The bed is **ours**.	Sally likes **us**.
You go to school.	This is **your** ball.	The bed is **yours**.	Sally likes **you**.
They go to school.	This is **their** ball.	The bed is **theirs**.	Sally likes **them**.

So kannst du jemanden nach etwas fragen:

Who is it?   Wer ist das?

What's this?   Was ist das?

What's your name?   Wie ist dein Name?

What's the weather like?   Wie ist das Wetter?

How are you?   Wie geht es dir?

How much is it?   Was kostet das?

How many ...?   Wie viel(e) ...?

When's your birthday?   Wann ist dein Geburtstag?

How old are you?   Wie alt bist du?

What time is it?   Wie spät ist es?

Can you ...?   Kannst du ...?

Do you like ...?   Magst du ...?

Can I have ...?   Kann ich ... haben?

Are you ...?   Bist du ...?

Have you got ...?   Hast du ...?

So kannst du etwas über dich und andere Dinge sagen:

I am/I am not ...   Ich bin/Ich bin nicht ...

I like/I don't like ...   Ich mag/Ich mag nicht ...

I have got/I haven't got ...   Ich habe/Ich habe nicht ...

I can/I can't ...   Ich kann/Ich kann nicht ...

I'd like to ...   Ich würde gern ...

This is ...   Das ist ...

It's ...   Es ist ...

It isn't ...   Es ist nicht ...

He/she/it is/isn't ...   Er/sie/es ist/ist nicht ...

He/she/it has/hasn't ...   Er/sie/es hat/hat nicht ...

He/she/it can/can't ...   Er/sie/es kann/kann nicht ...

My favourite ... is ...   Mein Lieblings-... ist ...

I'm from ...   Ich bin aus ...

I live in ...   Ich lebe in ...

I can speak ...   Ich spreche ...

My telephone number/address is ...   Meine Telefonnummer/Adresse ist ...

Wichtige Sätze und Fragen, die du in der Schule brauchst:

Can you help me, please?   Können Sie/Kannst du mir bitte helfen?

Can you say it again, please?   Können Sie/Kannst du das noch einmal sagen?

Sorry, I'm late.   Entschuldigung, ich bin zu spät.

Good morning.   Guten Morgen.

Goodbye.   Auf Wiedersehen.

What's … in German/English?   Was heißt … auf Deutsch/Englisch?

Give me …, please.   Gib mir bitte …

I've got a question.   Ich habe eine Frage.

Sorry, I don't understand.   Entschuldigung, ich verstehe nicht.

Can I go to the toilet?   Kann ich zur Toilette gehen?

Arbeitsaufträge, die du verstehen musst:

Listen.   Höre zu.

Read.   Lies.

Write.   Schreibe.

Draw./Draw lines.   Zeichne./Ziehe Linien.

Fill in.   Fülle aus.

Talk to …   Sprich mit …

Speak.   Sprich.

Play.   Spiele.

Circle.   Kreise ein.

Cut out.   Schneide aus.

Colour.   Male an.

Number.   Nummeriere.

Count.   Zähle.

Find.   Finde.

Find the correct order.   Finde die richtige Reihenfolge.

Match.   Verbinde.

Work with a partner/in groups.   Arbeite mit einem Partner./Arbeitet in der Gruppe.

Sing a song./Say a rhyme.   Sing ein Lied./Sag ein Gedicht.

Make.   Mache.

Create.   Erfinde./Bastle.

Present.   Präsentiere.

Point at/to …   Zeige auf …

Act out …   Spiele … vor.

Take (out) …   Nimm … (heraus).

Describe.   Beschreibe.

Words

A

actor, actress Schauspieler(in)
address Adresse
Afghanistan Afghanistan
Africa Afrika
in the afternoon am Nachmittag/
nachmittags
airport Flughafen
Albania Albanien
Albanian Albanisch
allergy Allergie
ambulance Krankenwagen
America Amerika
angel Engel
angry wütend, zornig
animal centre Tierheim
animal Tier
ankle Knöchel
anorak Anorak
apple Apfel
April April
Arabic Arabisch
architect Architekt(in)
arm Arm
armchair Sessel
artist Künstler(in)
(to do) arts and crafts basteln
arts Kunstunterricht
Asia Asien
assembly Versammlung
asthma Asthma
attic Speicher
August August
aunt Tante
Australia Australien
Austria Österreich
autumn Herbst

B

baby Baby
backache Rückenschmerzen
bacon Speck
baked beans eingemachte Bohnen
in Tomatensauce
ball Ball
(to do) ballet Ballett (tanzen)
balloon Ballon
banana Banane
bandage Verband
bank clerk Bankangestellte(r)
to bark bellen
basement Keller
basket Korb
basketball Basketball
(to play) basketball Basketball (spielen)
bathroom Badezimmer
bathtub Badewanne
beak Schnabel
bean Bohne
bear Bär
bed Bett
bedroom Schlafzimmer
bee Biene
beef Rindfleisch
behind hinter
beige beige
Belarus Weißrussland
Belgium Belgien
bell Glocke, Gong
belly Bauch
belly button Bauchnabel
belt Gürtel
to bend beugen
(best) friend (beste/r) Freund/in
between zwischen

big groß, hoch

bike Fahrrad

bikini Bikini

bill Rechnung

bird Vogel

birthday Geburtstag

biscuit Keks, Plätzchen

to bite beißen

bitter bitter

black schwarz

blackberry Brombeere

(black)board Tafel

to bleed bluten

blood Blut

blossom Blüte

blue blau

blueberry Blaubeere

board game Brettspiel

body Körper

boiled egg gekochtes Ei

bonfire Lagerfeuer

book Buch

bookshelf Bücherregal

boots Stiefel

boring langweilig

bowl Schale

Boxing Day 2. Weihnachtstag

boy Junge

brain Gehirn

Brazil Brasilien

bread Brot

to break Pause machen

breakfast Frühstück

to breathe atmen

broccoli Brokkoli

bronze bronzen, Bronze

broom Besen

brother Bruder

brown braun

brush Pinsel

to brush your teeth Zähne putzen

budgie Wellensittich

to build (a snowman) (einen Schneemann) bauen

to bump stoßen

to burn sich verbrennen

bus driver Busfahrer/in

butter Butter

butterfly Schmetterling

button Knopf

to buy kaufen

to buy a ticket eine Fahrkarte kaufen

C

cabbage Kohl

cage Käfig

cake Kuchen

to calculate rechnen

calendar Kalender

camel Kamel

campfire Lagerfeuer

Canada Kanada

candle Kerze

candy Süßigkeit

cap Kappe, Mütze

car Auto

card Karte

carpet Teppich

carrot Karotte

cart Einkaufswagen

cash desk Kasse

cashier Kassierer(in)

cast Gips

castle Burg

cat Katze

cauliflower   Blumenkohl

cellar   Keller

cereal   Getreideflocken

chair   Stuhl

chalk   Kreide

to change   umsteigen, wechseln

cheap   billig

Chechen   Tschetschenisch

Chechenia   Tschetschenien

cheeks   Wangen

cheese   Käse

cheeseburger   Cheeseburger

cherry   Kirsche

chick   Küken

chicken and chips   Hühnchen mit
Pommes frites

chickenpox   Windpocken

children   Kinder

chimney   Schornstein

chin   Kinn

China   China

Chinese   Chinesisch

to chirp   zwitschern

chocolate   Schokolade

chocolate bar   Schokoriegel

chocolate milk, hot chocolate   kalter/
heißer Kakao

choir   Chor

to choose   aussuchen

Christ Child   Christkind

Christmas   Weihnachten

Christmas baubles
Weihnachtsbaumkugeln

Christmas card   Weihnachtskarte

Christmas carol   Weihnachtslied

Christmas cracker
Weihnachtsknallbonbon

Christmas Day   1. Weihnachtstag

Christmas dinner   Weihnachtsessen

Christmas Eve   Heiligabend

Christmas holidays   Weihnachtsferien

Christmas market   Weihnachtsmarkt

Christmas tree   Weihnachtsbaum

chubby   pummelig

to cluck   gackern

cinema   Kino

to circle   einkreisen

to clap   klatschen

class   Klasse

classroom   Klassenzimmer

claw   Kralle

to clean   putzen

clever   schlau

to climb   klettern

clothes   Kleidung

clothes shop   Kleiderladen

cloud   Wolke

cloudy   wolkig

coat   Mantel

cobweb   Spinnennetz

coffee   Kaffee

coffee to go   Kaffee zum Mitnehmen

coin   Münze

coke   Cola

cold   kalt, Erkältung, Schnupfen

collar   Kragen

to collect cards/stickers   Karten/Sticker
sammeln

colour   Farbe

to colour   färben, ausmalen, anmalen

coloured   farbig

colourful   bunt

computer game   Computerspiel

continent   Kontinent

continental breakfast kontinentales, kleines Frühstück

to cook kochen

cooker Herd

cookie Keks

to cool kühlen

corner Ecke

cornflakes Cornflakes

corridor Flur

costume Kostüm

cough Husten

to count zählen

to count backwards rückwärts zählen

to count forward vorwärts zählen

to count from … to … von … nach … zählen

country Land

cousin Cousin/e

cow Kuh

cream Sahne

cream cheese Frischkäse

to croak quaken

Croatia Kroatien

Croatian Kroatisch

crocodile Krokodil

crown Krone

cucumber Gurke

cuddly toy Kuscheltier

cup Tasse

cupboard Schrank

currant Johannisbeere

customer Kunde(in)

to cut schneiden

cutlery Besteck

Czech Tschechisch

Czech Republic Tschechische Republik

D

dad, daddy Papa

to dance tanzen

dangerous gefährlich

Danish Dänisch

dark dunkel

dark blue dunkelblau

daughter Tochter

day Tag

days of the week Wochentage

dead tot

December Dezember

to decorate dekorieren

decorated dekoriert

delayed verspätet

delicious köstlich

Denmark Dänemark

dentist Zahnarzt/-ärztin

designer Designer(in)

desk Schreibtisch

dessert Nachtisch

diarrhea Durchfall

dining room Esszimmer

to dive tauchen

divorced geschieden

to do maths rechnen

to do sports Sport treiben

to do your homework Hausaufgaben machen

doctor Arzt/Ärztin

dog Hund

doll Puppe

dollar Dollar

dolphin Delfin

donkey Esel

door Tür

double-decker bus Doppeldeckerbus

to draw   zeichnen

to dream   träumen

dress   Kleid

to dress up   sich verkleiden

to drink   trinken

drinks stand   Getränkestand

to drive   fahren

drop   Bonbon

(to play the) drums   Schlagzeug (spielen)

dry   trocken

duck   Ente

Dutch   Holländisch

E

eagle   Adler

ear   Ohr

earache   Ohrenschmerzen

to earn money   Geld verdienen

Easter bunny   Osterhase

Easter egg   Osterei

Easter Monday   Ostermontag

Easter Sunday   Ostersonntag

to eat   essen, fressen

egg   Ei

Egypt   Ägypten

eight   acht

eighteen   achtzehn

eighty   achtzig

elbow   Ellbogen

electrician   Elektriker(in)

elephant   Elefant

eleven   elf

elk   Elch

empty   leer

engineer   Ingenieur(in)

English   Englisch

Estonia   Estland

Estonian   Estnisch

euro   Euro

Europe   Europa

in the evening   am Abend/abends

to examine   untersuchen, behandeln

exiting   aufregend

expensive   teuer

eye   Auge

eyebrow   Augenbraue

eyelashes   Wimpern

F

face   Gesicht

family member   Familienmitglied

family tree   Stammbaum

farm   Bauernhof

farmer   Bauer/Bäuerin

fast   schnell

fat   dick, fett

father   Vater

Father Christmas, Santa Claus

Weihnachtsmann

feather   Feder

February   Februar

to feed   füttern

to feed (the cat, ...)   (die Katze, ...)

füttern

fence   Zaun

ferry   Fähre

fifteen   fünfzehn

fifty   fünfzig

to fill in   ausfüllen

fin   Flosse

fine   gut

fineliner   Fineliner

finger   Finger

fingernail   Fingernagel

Finland   Finnland
Finnish   Finnisch
firefighter   Feuerwehrmann/-frau
fireplace   (offener) Kamin
first floor   erster Stock
first name   Vorname
fish, fish   Fisch, Fische
fit   fit
five   fünf
flamingo   Flamingo
to flash   (auf)blitzen
flat   Wohnung
flight attendant   Flugbegleiter(in)
floor   Etage, Stockwerk
flower   Blume
flu   Grippe
fly   Fliege
to fly   fliegen
foal   Fohlen
fog   Nebel
foggy   neblig
to fold   falten
folder   Schnellhefter
foot, feet   Fuß, Füße
football   Fußball
(to play) football   Fußball (spielen)
football player   Footballspieler(in)
forehead   Stirn
fork   Gabel
forty   vierzig
four   vier
fourteen   vierzehn
fox   Fuchs
France   Frankreich
French   Französisch
Friday   Freitag
fridge (refrigerator)   Kühlschrank
fried egg   Spiegelei

friend   Freund/in
friendship   Freundschaft
to be frightened   Angst haben
frisbee   Frisbee
frog   Frosch
fruit   Frucht, Obst
fruit salad   Obstsalat
fruity   fruchtig
full   voll
funny   komisch, lustig
fur   Fell
furniture   Möbel

G

game console   Spielekonsole
garage   Garage
garden   Garten
garlic   Knoblauch
Georgia   Georgien
Georgian   Georgisch
German   Deutsch
German measles   Röteln
Germany   Deutschland
to get (a present)   (ein Geschenk) bekommen
to get dressed   sich anziehen
to get off   aussteigen
to get on   einsteigen
to get up   aufstehen
ghost   Geist, Gespenst
gingerbread   Honigkuchen
giraffe   Giraffe
girl   Mädchen
to give milk   Milch geben
glass   Glas
gloves   Handschuhe
glue stick   Klebestift

to go for a walk   spazieren gehen

to go home   nach Hause gehen

to go out for...   ausgehen zum ...

to go to bed   zu Bett gehen

to go to school   zur Schule gehen

goat   Ziege

godfather   Pate

godmother   Patin

gold   golden, Gold

goldfish   Goldfisch

Good Friday   Karfreitag

goose, geese   Gans, Gänse

gorilla   Gorilla

grandfather   Großvater

grandma, granny   Oma

grandmother   Großmutter

grandpa   Opa

grandparents   Großeltern

grape   Traube

Great Britain   Großbritannien

great-grandmother   Urgroßmutter

Greece   Griechenland

Greek   Griechisch

green   grün

grey   grau

grizzly (bear)   Grizzly(-bär)

ground floor   Erdgeschoss

guard   Wache

guest   Gast

guinea pig   Meerschweinchen

guitar   Gitarre

(to play the) guitar   Gitarre (spielen)

H

hair   Haar

hairdresser   Friseur(in)

ham   Schinken

hamburger   Hamburger

hamster   Hamster

hand   Hand

to hang up   aufhängen

Happy Easter   Frohe Ostern

happy   glücklich

hat   Hut

to haunt   spuken

haunted castle   Spukschloss

to have a bath   ein Bad nehmen/baden

to have breakfast   frühstücken

to have dinner   zu Abend essen

to have lunch   zu Mittag essen

hay   Heu

head   Kopf

headache   Kopfschmerzen

heart   Herz

heat   Hitze

Hebrew   Hebräisch

helicopter   Hubschrauber

helmet   Helm

to help   helfen

to help in the kitchen/garden/house

in der Küche/im Garten/im Haus helfen

hen   Huhn

to hide   verstecken

hip   Hüfte

hippo   Nilpferd

hobby, hobbies   Hobby, Hobbys

(to play) hockey   Hockey (spielen)

holidays   Ferien

holy night   Heilige Nacht

at home   zu Hause

homework   Hausaufgabe

honey   Honig

hood   Kapuze

hoodie   Kapuzenpullover

hoof, hooves   Huf, Hufe

horse   Pferd
hospital   Krankenhaus
hot dog   Hotdog
hot   heiß
house   Haus
hundred   hundert
Hungarian   Ungarisch
Hungary   Ungarn
hungry   hungrig
to hunt   jagen
hurricane   Wirbelsturm
to hurt   weh tun
husband   Ehemann

I

ice cream   Eis(krem)
ice cream stand   Eiskremstand
iced tea   Eistee
to ice-skate   Schlittschuh fahren
icy   eisig
in   in
in front of   vor
incense   Weihrauch
injection   Spritze
ink cartridge   Tintenpatrone
ink eraser   Tintenkiller
to inline skate   Inlineskates fahren
inline skates   Inlineskates
(to play an) instrument   ein Instrument (spielen)
invitation   Einladung
Iran   Iran
Iraq   Irak
Ireland   Irland
Israel   Israel
Italian   Italienisch
Italy   Italien

J

jacket   Jacke
jack-o'-lantern   Kürbislaterne
jam   Marmelade
January   Januar
Japan   Japan
Japanese   Japanisch
jeans   Jeans
jeans shop   Jeansladen
jingle bells   Klingglöckchen
job   Beruf, Aufgabe
jobless   arbeitslos
jogging suit   Jogginganzug
journalist   Journalist(in)
judge   Richter(in)
(to do) judo   Judo (machen)
juice   Saft
July   Juli
to jump   springen
jumper   Pulli
jumpsuit   Overall
June   Juni
jungle   Dschungel

K

kale   Grünkohl
kangaroo   Känguru
(to do) karate   Karate (machen)
ketchup   Ketchup
king   König
kiosk   Kiosk
kitchen   Küche
kite   Drachen
kitten   Kätzchen
kiwi   Kiwi
knee   Knie

knife, knives   Messer, Messer

to knock   klopfen

koala (bear)   Koala(-bär)

L

lamp   Lampe

language   Sprache

late   spät

Latvia   Lettland

Latvian   Lettisch

lawyer   Rechtsanwalt/-anwältin

to lay eggs   Eier legen

to learn   lernen

leek   Lauch

left   links

left-hand traffic   Linksverkehr

leg   Bein

lemon   Zitrone

letterbox   Briefkasten

lettuce   Salat

light   hell

light blue   hellblau

lightning   Blitz

lion   Löwe

to listen   zuhören

to listen to music   Musik hören

literacy   Lesen und Schreiben

Lithuania   Litauen

Lithuanian   Litauisch

little   klein

to live   leben

living room   Wohnzimmer

lollipop   Lutscher

long   lang

lorry   LKW

loud   laut

to love   lieben

lunch   Mittagessen

M

to make my bed   mein Bett machen

manager   Manager(in)

mane   Mähne

manger   Krippe

map   (Land-)Karte

March   März

market   Markt

marmalade   Orangenmarmelade

married   verheiratet

mashed potatoes   Kartoffelbrei

mask   Maske

to match   zuordnen

maths   Mathe

May   Mai

mayonnaise   Mayonnaise

measles   Masern

meat   Fleisch

mechanic   Mechaniker(in)

(medical) doctor   Arzt/Ärztin

medicine   Medikament

to meet   treffen

melon   Melone

menu   Speisekarte

midnight   Mitternacht

milk   Milch

million   Million

millionaire   Millionär(in)

mince pie   Minzpastete

mistletoe   Mistel(zweig)

mobile (phone)   Handy

Monday   Montag

money   Geld

monkey   Affe

monster   Monster

month   Monat

to moo   muhen

moon   Mond
in the morning   am Morgen/morgens
mother   Mutter
mountain bike   Mountainbike
mouse, mice   Maus, Mäuse
mouth   Mund
to move   umziehen
MP4 player   MP4-Player
muesli   Müsli
mug   Becher
mum, mummy   Mama
mummy   Mumie
mushroom   Pilz
music   Musik
music shop   Musikgeschäft
musician   Musiker(in)
mustard   Senf
myrrh   Myrrhe

N

name   Name
napkin   Serviette
nationality   Nationalität
neck   Hals
neckache   Nackenschmerzen
to neigh   wiehern
nephew   Neffe
Netherlands   Niederlande
new   neu
New Zealand   Neuseeland
next to   neben
nickname   Spitzname
niece   Nichte
night   Nacht
at night   in der Nacht/nachts
nine   neun
nineteen   neunzehn
ninety   neunzig

noon   Mittag
Norway   Norwegen
Norwegian   Norwegisch
nose   Nase
November   November
number   Zahl
nurse   Krankenschwester/
Krankenpfleger
nursery teacher   Kindergärtner(in)
nut   Nuss
nutcracker   Nussknacker

O

oats   Hafer
October   Oktober
old   alt
on   auf
on time   pünktlich
one   eins
onion   Zwiebel
to open   öffnen
operation   Operation
orange   orange, Orange, Apfelsine
orange juice   Orangensaft
owl   Eule

PQ

to paint   malen
painter   Maler(in)
a pair of   ein Paar
a pair of trousers   Hose
palace   Schloss
pancake   Pfannkuchen
parcel   Paket, Päckchen
parents   Eltern
parrot   Papagei
partner   Lebensgefährte/in

party   Party, Feier

Pashto   Paschtunisch

passport   (Reise-)Pass

patient   Patient

to pay   bezahlen

pea   Erbse

pear   Birne

pedestrian   Fußgänger

to peel   schälen

pen   Füller, Fineliner

pence   Pence

pencil   Bleistift

pencil case   Federmäppchen

pencil sharpener   Spitzer

pencils   Stifte

penguin   Pinguin

penny   Penny

pepper   Paprika, Pfeffer

Persian   Persisch

pet   Haustier

pharmacy   Apotheke

(to play the) piano   Klavier (spielen)

pig   Schwein

piglet   Ferkel

pill   Tablette

pilot   Pilot(in)

pineapple   Ananas

pink   rosa, pink

pizza   Pizza

plane   Flugzeug

plaster   Pflaster

plate   Teller

platform   Bahnsteig

to play   spielen

to play a trick   Streich spielen

to play with friends   mit Freunden spielen

playground   Pausenhof, Spielplatz

playing cards   Spielkarten

plum   Pflaume

plum pudding   Plumpudding

plumber   Klempner(in)

Poland   Polen

polar bear   Eisbär

policeman/-woman   Polizist(in)

Polish   Polnisch

pork   Schweinefleisch

porridge   Haferbrei

Portugal   Portugal

Portuguese   Portugiesisch

poster   Poster

postman   Briefträger

potato, potatoes   Kartoffel, Kartoffeln

pound   Pfund

to pour   eingießen

prescription   Rezept

present   Geschenk

price tag   Preisschild

prince   Prinz

princess   Prinzessin

products   Produkte

programmer   Programmierer(in)

pudding   Pudding

to pull   ziehen

pullover   Pullover

pumpkin   Kürbis

pupil   Schüler(in)

puppy   Welpe

purple   lila

to put away   wegräumen

to put on   anziehen

pyjamas   Schlafanzug

queen   Königin

quiet   leise

R

rabbit   Kaninchen

racing car   Rennauto

radish   Radieschen

rain   Regen

to rain   regnen

rainbow   Regenbogen

raincoat   Regenmantel

rainy   regnerisch

raspberry   Himbeere

rat   Ratte

to read   lesen

to read a book   ein Buch lesen

(to play the) recorder   Blockflöte (spielen)

red   rot

refugee   Flüchtling

reindeer, reindeer   Rentier, Rentiere

relatives   Verwandte

remote controlled car   ferngesteuertes Auto

to repair   reparieren

reporter   Reporter

restaurant   Restaurant

rhino   Nashorn

ribbon   Band

rice   Reis

to ride a bike   Fahrrad fahren

to ride a horse   reiten

right   rechts

right-hand traffic   Rechtsverkehr

to ring the doorbell   an der Tür klingeln

River Thames   Themse

road   Straße

to roar   brüllen

roll   Brötchen

room   Zimmer, Raum

Royal Family   Königliche Familie

rubber   Radiergummi

ruler   Lineal

Romania   Rumänien

Romanian   Rumänisch

to run   rennen, laufen

Russia   Russland

Russian   Russisch

S

sad   traurig

salad   Salat

salt   Salz

sandals   Sandalen

sandbox   Sandkasten

sandwich   Sandwich

Saturday   Samstag

sausage   Würstchen

(to play the) saxophone   Saxophon (spielen)

scared   verängstigt, erschrocken

to be scared   Angst haben

scarf   Schal

scary   gruselig

school   Schule

school subject   Schulfach

school things   Schulsachen

school uniform   Schuluniform

schoolbag   Schultasche

schoolbus   Schulbus

schoolyard   Schulhof

science   Naturwissenschaft

scissors   Schere

scoop   Eiskugel

scooter   Roller, Vespa

scrambled egg   Rührei

seal   Robbe, Seehund

seasons   Jahreszeiten

second floor   zweiter Stock

September   September

seven   sieben

seventeen   siebzehn

seventy   siebzig

to shake   schütteln

shark   Hai(-fisch)

sheep, sheep   Schaf, Schafe

shelves   Regal

to shine   leuchten

shiny   leuchtend

ship   Schiff

shirt   Hemd

shoe shop   Schuhgeschäft

shoes   Schuhe

shop   Geschäft, Laden

shop assistant   Verkäufer(in)

shopping bag   Einkaufstasche

shopping centre   Einkaufszentrum

shopping list   Einkaufsliste

short   kurz

shorts   Shorts

shoulder   Schulter

shower   Dusche

siblings   Geschwister

sick   krank, übel

silver   silbern, Silber

to sing   singen

to sing in a choir   im Chor singen

singer   Sänger(in)

single mum/dad   alleinerziehende/r
Mutter/Vater

sister   Schwester

six   sechs

sixteen   sechzehn

sixty   sechzig

skateboard   Skateboard

to skateboard   Skateboard fahren

skeleton   Skelett

to skip rope   Seil springen

skipping rope   Springseil

skirt   Rock

sky   Himmel

to sleep   schlafen

sleigh   Schlitten

slide   Rutsche

slow   langsam

small   klein

smartphone   Smartphone

smoothie   Smoothie, Fruchtshake

snake   Schlange

to snap (your fingers)   (mit den Fingern)
schnippen

sneakers   Turnschuhe

snow   Schnee

to snow   schneien

snowboard   Snowboard

to snowboard   snowboarden

snowman   Schneemann

snowy   verschneit

socks   Socken

sofa   Sofa

son   Sohn

sore throat   Halsschmerzen

soup   Suppe

sour   sauer

spaceship   Raumschiff

spaghetti   Spaghetti

Spain   Spanien

Spanish   Spanisch

to speak   sprechen

spider   Spinne

spider's web   Spinnennetz

spinach   Spinat

spoon   Löffel

sports   Sport
sports shop   Sportgeschäft
sports star   Sportstar
spouse   Ehepartner/in
spring   Frühling
to squeak   quieken
squirrel   Eichhörnchen
stable   Stall
stairs   Treppe
to stamp   stampfen
star   Stern
station   Bahnhof, Haltestelle
stepbrother   Stiefbruder
stepfather   Stiefvater
stepmother   Stiefmutter
stepsister   Stiefschwester
stickers   Aufkleber
stilts   Stelzen
stocking   Strumpf
stomachache   Bauchweh
store   Kaufhaus
storm   Sturm
to storm   stürmen
straw   Stroh
strawberry   Erdbeere
street   Straße
strong   stark
to study   lernen
stupid   dumm
sugar   Zucker
summer   Sommer
sun   Sonne
Sunday   Sonntag
sunny   sonnig
supermarket   Supermarkt
surname   Nachname
sweater   Pulli

sweet   süß
sweets   Süßigkeiten
sweet shop   Süßwarenladen
to swim   schwimmen
swimming pool   Schwimmbecken
swimming trunks   Badehose
swimsuit   Badeanzug
swing   Schaukel
Switzerland   Schweiz
Syria   Syrien
syrup   Sirup

T

table   Tisch
tablet   Tablet
tail   Schwanz
to take (the bus)   (den Bus) nehmen
to take a shower   duschen
to take off   ausziehen
to take out   herausnehmen
to take the dog for a walk   den Hund ausführen
tall   hoch, groß
to taste   probieren
tasty   lecker
taxi   Taxi
tea   Tee
teacher   Lehrer(in)
technician   Techniker(in)
teddy bear   Teddybär
temperature   Temperatur
to have a temperature   Fieber haben
ten   zehn
(to play) tennis   Tennis (spielen)
Thanksgiving Day   Erntedankfest
thermometer   Thermometer
thigh   Oberschenkel

thin   dünn

thirsty   durstig

thirteen   dreizehn

thirty   dreißig

thousand   tausend

three   drei

thunder   Donner

to thunder   donnern

thunderstorm   Gewitter

Thursday   Donnerstag

to tick   abhaken

ticket   Fahrkarte

to tidy my room   mein Zimmer aufräumen

to tidy up   aufräumen

tie   Krawatte

tiger   Tiger

tights   Strumpfhose

timetable   Fahrplan

tired   müde

tissues   Taschentücher

toast   Toast

today   heute

toe   Zeh

toenail   Zehennagel

toilet   Toilette

tomato, tomatoes   Tomate, Tomaten

tomato sauce   Tomatensoße

tomorrow   morgen

tonight   heute Abend

too big   zu groß

too old   zu alt

too small   zu klein

tooth, teeth   Zahn, Zähne

toothache   Zahnschmerzen

tortoise   (Land-)Schildkröte

to touch   berühren

towel   Handtuch

toy shop   Spielwarenladen

traditional English breakfast   englisches Frühstück

traffic jam   Verkehrsstau

traffic light   Ampel

train   Zug

trainers   Turnschuhe

tram   Straßenbahn

transport   Transport

to travel   reisen

tray   Tablett

Trick or treat!   Süßes oder Saures!

(to play the) trumpet   Trompete (spielen)

trunk   Rüssel

to try on   anprobieren

T-shirt   T-Shirt

Tuesday   Dienstag

turkey   Truthahn

Turkey   Türkei

Turkish   Türkisch

turtle   Wasserschildkröte

TV (television)   Fernseher

twelve   zwölf

twenty   zwanzig

twins   Zwillinge

two   zwei

U

uncle   Onkel

under   unter

underground   U-Bahn

to understand   verstehen

underwear   Unterwäsche

to unwrap   auspacken

USA   USA

V

Valentine's Day   Valentinstag

vampire   Vampir

vanilla   Vanille

vegetables   Gemüse

vegetarian   vegetarisch

vest   Weste

vet   Tierarzt/-ärztin

violet   violett

(to play the) violin   Geige (spielen)

(to play) volleyball   Volleyball (spielen)

to vomit   sich übergeben

W

waggon   Wagen

to wait   warten

waiter, waitress   Kellner(in)

waiting room   Wartezimmer

to walk   gehen, laufen

to walk the dog   den Hund ausführen

to want   wollen

wardrobe   Kleiderschrank

warm   warm

to wash   waschen

to wash your hands   Hände waschen

washbasin   Waschbecken

waste-paper basket   Papierkorb

to watch TV   fernsehen

water   Wasser

watermelon   Wassermelone

water-tap   Wasserhahn

to wear   tragen

weather   Wetter

weather forecast   Wettervorhersage

Wednesday   Mittwoch

week   Woche

weekend   Wochenende

wellies (wellingtons)   Gummistiefel

wet   nass

wheelchair   Rollstuhl

white   weiß

whiteboard   Whiteboard

wife   Ehefrau

wind   Wind

window   Fenster

windy   windig

wing   Flügel

winter   Winter

to wish (for)   sich wünschen

wish list   Wunschzettel

witch, witches   Hexe, Hexen

wolf   Wolf

woolly hat   Mütze

to work   arbeiten

world   Welt

wound   Wunde

wrapping paper   Geschenkpapier

to write   schreiben

XYZ

year   Jahr

yellow   gelb

yesterday   gestern

yoghurt   Joghurt

young   jung

zebra   Zebra

zebra crossing   Zebrastreifen

zipper   Reißverschluss

zoo   Zoo

zookeeper   Tierpfleger(in)

A

am Abend/abends   in the evening

zu Abend essen   to have dinner

abhaken   to tick

acht   eight

achtzehn   eighteen

achtzig   eighty

Adler   eagle

Adresse   address

Affe   monkey

Afghanistan   Afghanistan

Afrika   Africa

Ägypten   Egypt

Albanien   Albania

Albanisch   Albanian

alleinerziehende/r Mutter/Vater   single mum/dad

Allergie   allergy

alt   old

Amerika   America

Ampel   traffic light

an der Tür klingeln   to ring the doorbell

Ananas   pineapple

Angst haben   to be frightened, to be scared

anmalen   to colour

Anorak   anorak

anprobieren   to try on

anziehen   to put on

sich anziehen   to get dressed

Apfel   apple

Apfelsine   orange

Apotheke   pharmacy

April   April

Arabisch   Arabic

arbeiten   to work

arbeitslos   jobless

Architekt(in)   architect

Arm   arm

Arzt/Ärztin   (medical) doctor

Asien   Asia

Asthma   asthma

atmen   to breathe

auf   on

(auf)blitzen   to flash

Aufgabe   job

aufhängen   to hang up

Aufkleber   stickers

aufräumen   to tidy up

aufregend   exiting

aufstehen   to get up

Auge   eye

Augenbraue   eyebrow

August   August

ausfüllen   to fill in

ausgehen zum …   to go out for…

ausmalen   to colour

auspacken   to unwrap

aussteigen   to get off

aussuchen   to choose

Australien   Australia

ausziehen   to take off

Auto   car

B

Baby   baby

ein Bad nehmen/baden   to have a bath

Badeanzug   swimsuit

Badehose   swimming trunks

Badewanne   bathtub

Badezimmer   bathroom

Bahnhof   station

Bahnsteig   platform

Ball   ball

Ballett (tanzen)   (to do) ballet

Ballon   balloon
Banane   banana
Band   ribbon
Bankangestellte(r)   bank clerk
Bär   bear
Basketball   basketball
Basketball (spielen)   (to play) basketball
basteln   (to do) arts and crafts
Bauch   belly
Bauchnabel   belly button
Bauchweh   stomachache
(einen Schneemann) bauen   to build (a snowman)
Bauer/Bäuerin   farmer
Bauernhof   farm
Becher   mug
behandeln   to examine
beige   beige
Bein   leg
beißen   to bite
(ein Geschenk) bekommen   to get (a present)
Belgien   Belgium
bellen   to bark
Beruf   job
berühren   to touch
Besen   broom
Besteck   cutlery
(beste/r) Freund/in   (best) friend
Bett   bed
zu Bett gehen   to go to bed
beugen   to bend
bezahlen   to pay
Biene   bee
Bikini   bikini
billig   cheap
Birne   pear
bitter   bitter

blau   blue
Blaubeere   blueberry
Bleistift   pencil
Blitz   lightning
Blockflöte (spielen)   (to play the) recorder
Blume   flower
Blumenkohl   cauliflower
Blut   blood
Blüte   blossom
bluten   to bleed
Bohne   bean
Bonbon   drop
Brasilien   Brazil
braun   brown
Brettspiel   board game
Briefkasten   letterbox
Briefträger   postman
Brokkoli   broccoli
Brombeere   blackberry
bronzen, Bronze   bronze
Brot   bread
Brötchen   roll
Bruder   brother
brüllen   to roar
Buch   book
ein Buch lesen   to read a book
Bücherregal   bookshelf
bunt   colourful
Burg   castle
Busfahrer/in   bus driver
Butter   butter

C

Cheeseburger   cheeseburger
China   China
Chinesisch   Chinese

Chor   choir
im Chor singen   to sing in a choir
Christkind   Christ Child
Cola   coke
Computerspiel   computer game
Cornflakes   cornflakes
Cousin/e   cousin

D

Dänemark   Denmark
Dänisch   Danish
Dezember   December
dekorieren   to decorate
dekoriert   decorated
Delfin   dolphin
Designer(in)   designer
Deutsch   German
Deutschland   Germany
dick   fat
Dienstag   Tuesday
Dollar   dollar
Donner   thunder
donnern   to thunder
Donnerstag   Thursday
Doppeldeckerbus   double-decker bus
Drachen   kite
drei   three
dreißig   thirty
dreizehn   thirteen
Dschungel   jungle
dumm   stupid
dunkel   dark
dunkelblau   dark blue
dünn   thin
Durchfall   diarrhea
durstig   thirsty
Dusche   shower
duschen   to take a shower

E

Ecke   corner
Ehefrau   wife
Ehemann   husband
Ehepartner/in   spouse
Ei   egg
Eichhörnchen   squirrel
Eier legen   to lay eggs
eingemachte Bohnen in Tomatensauce
baked beans
eingießen   to pour
Einkaufsliste   shopping list
Einkaufstasche   shopping bag
Einkaufswagen   cart
Einkaufszentrum   shopping centre
einkreisen   to circle
Einladung   invitation
eins   one
einsteigen   to get on
Eis(krem)   ice cream
Eisbär   polar bear
eisig   icy
Eiskremstand   ice cream stand
Eiskugel   scoop
Eistee   iced tea
Elch   elk
Elefant   elephant
Elektriker(in)   electrician
elf   eleven
Ellbogen   elbow
Eltern   parents
Engel   angel
Englisch   English
englisches Frühstück   traditional
English breakfast
Ente   duck
Erbse   pea

Erdbeere   strawberry
Erdgeschoss   ground floor
Erkältung   cold
Erntedankfest   Thanksgiving Day
erschrocken   scared
erster Stock   first floor
Erster Weihnachtstag   Christmas Day
Esel   donkey
essen   to eat
Esszimmer   dining room
Estland   Estonia
Estnisch   Estonian
Etage   floor
Eule   owl
Euro   euro
Europa   Europe

F

Fähre   ferry
fahren   to drive
Fahrkarte   ticket
eine Fahrkarte kaufen   to buy a ticket
Fahrplan   timetable
Fahrrad   bike
Fahrrad fahren   to ride a bike
falten   to fold
Familienmitglied   family member
Farbe   colour
färben   to colour
farbig   coloured
Februar   February
Feder   feather
Federmäppchen   pencil case
Feier   party
Fell   fur
Fenster   window
Ferien   holidays

Ferkel   piglet
ferngesteuertes Auto   remote controlled car
fernsehen   to watch TV
Fernseher   TV (television)
fett   fat
Feuerwehrmann/-frau   firefighter
Fieber haben   to have a temperature
Fineliner   fineliner, pen
Finger   finger
Fingernagel   fingernail
Finnisch   Finnish
Finnland   Finland
Fisch, Fische   fish, fish
fit   fit
Flamingo   flamingo
Fleisch   meat
Fliege   fly
fliegen   to fly
Flosse   fin
Flüchtling   refugee
Flugbegleiter(in)   flight attendant
Flügel   wing
Flughafen   airport
Flugzeug   plane
Flur   corridor
Fohlen   foal
Footballspieler(in)   football player
Frankreich   France
Französisch   French
fressen   to eat
Freund/in   friend
Freundschaft   friendship
Freitag   Friday
Frisbee   frisbee
Frischkäse   cream cheese
Friseur(in)   hairdresser
Frohe Ostern   Happy Easter

Frosch   frog
Frucht   fruit
fruchtig   fruity
Fruchtshake   smoothie
Frühling   spring
Frühstück   breakfast
frühstücken   to have breakfast
Fuchs   fox
Füller   pen
fünf   five
fünfzehn   fifteen
fünfzig   fifty
Fuß, Füße   foot, feet
Fußball   football
Fußball (spielen)   (to play) football
Fußgänger   pedestrian
füttern   to feed
(die Katze, …) füttern   to feed
(the cat, …)

G

Gabel   fork
gackern   to cluck
Gans, Gänse   goose, geese
Garage   garage
Garten   garden
Gast   guest
Geburtstag   Birthday
gefährlich   dangerous
gehen   to walk
Gehirn   brain
Geige (spielen)   (to play the) violin
Geist   ghost
gekochtes Ei   boiled egg
gelb   yellow
Geld   money
Geld verdienen   to earn money

Gemüse   vegetables
Georgien   Georgia
Georgisch   Georgian
Geschäft   shop
Geschenk   present
Geschenkpapier   wrapping paper
geschieden   divorced
Geschwister   siblings
Gesicht   face
Gespenst   ghost
gestern   yesterday
Getränkestand   drinks stand
Getreideflocken   cereal
Gewitter   thunderstorm
Gips   cast
Giraffe   giraffe
Gitarre   guitar
Gitarre (spielen)   (to play the) guitar
Glas   glass
Glocke   bell
glücklich   happy
golden, Gold   gold
Goldfisch   goldfish
Gong   bell
Gorilla   gorilla
grau   grey
Griechenland   Greece
Griechisch   Greek
Grippe   flu
Grizzly(-bär)   grizzly (bear)
groß   big, tall
Großbritannien   Great Britain
Großeltern   grandparents
Großmutter   grandmother
Großvater   grandfather
grün   green
Grünkohl   kale
gruselig   scary

Gummistiefel   wellies (wellingtons)
Gurke   cucumber
Gürtel   belt
gut   fine

Haar   hair
Hafer   oats
Haferbrei   porridge
Hai(-fisch)   shark
Hals   neck
Halsschmerzen   sore throat
Haltestelle   station
Hamburger   hamburger
Hamster   hamster
Hand   hand
Hände waschen   to wash your hands
Handschuhe   gloves
Handtuch   towel
Handy   mobile (phone)
Haus   house
Hausaufgabe   homework
Hausaufgaben machen   to do your
homework
Haustier   pet
Hebräisch   Hebrew
Heiligabend   Christmas Eve
Heilige Nacht   holy night
heiß   hot
helfen   to help
hell   light
hellblau   light blue
Helm   helmet
Hemd   shirt
herausnehmen   to take out
Herbst   autumn
Herd   cooker

Herz   heart
Heu   hay
heute   today
heute Abend   tonight
Hexe, Hexen   witch, witches
Himbeere   raspberry
Himmel   sky
hinter   behind
Hitze   heat
Hobby, Hobbys   hobby, hobbies
hoch   big, tall
Hockey (spielen)   (to play) hockey
Holländisch   Dutch
Honig   honey
Honigkuchen   gingerbread
Hose   a pair of trousers
Hotdog   hot dog
Hubschrauber   helicopter
Huf, Hufe   hoof, hooves
Hüfte   hip
Huhn   hen
Hühnchen mit Pommes frites   chicken
and chips
Hund   dog
den Hund ausführen   to walk the dog/to
take the dog for a walk
hundert   hundred
hungrig   hungry
Husten   cough
Hut   hat

in   in
in der Küche/im Garten/im Haus helfen
to help in the kitchen/garden/house
Ingenieur(in)   engineer
Inlineskates fahren   to inline skate

Inlineskates   inline skates
ein Instrument (spielen)   (to play an) instrument
Irak   Iraq
Iran   Iran
Irland   Ireland
Israel   Israel
Italien   Italy
Italienisch   Italian

J

Jacke   jacket
jagen   to hunt
Jahr   year
Jahreszeiten   seasons
Januar   January
Japan   Japan
Japanisch   Japanese
Jeans   jeans
Jeansladen   jeans shop
Jogginganzug   jogging suit
Joghurt   yoghurt
Johannisbeere   currant
Journalist(in)   journalist
Judo (machen)   (to do) judo
Juli   July
Juni   June
jung   young
Junge   boy

K

Kaffee   coffee
Kaffee zum Mitnehmen   coffee to go
Käfig   cage
Kalender   calendar
kalt   cold

kalter/heißer Kakao   chocolate milk, hot chocolate
Kamel   camel
(offener) Kamin   fireplace
Kanada   Canada
Känguru   kangaroo
Kaninchen   rabbit
Kappe   cap
Kapuze   hood
Kapuzenpullover   hoodie
Karate (machen)   (to do) karate
Karfreitag   Good Friday
Karotte   carrot
Karte   card, map
Karten/Sticker sammeln   to collect cards/stickers
Kartoffel, Kartoffeln   potato, potatoes
Kartoffelbrei   mashed potatoes
Käse   cheese
Kasse   cash desk
Kassierer(in)   cashier
Kätzchen   kitten
Katze   cat
kaufen   to buy
Kaufhaus   store
Keks   cookie, biscuit
Keller   cellar, basement
Kellner(in)   waiter, waitress
Kerze   candle
Ketchup   ketchup
Kinder   children
Kindergärtner(in)   nursery teacher
Kinn   chin
Kino   cinema
Kiosk   kiosk
Kirsche   cherry
Kiwi   kiwi
Klasse   class

Klassenzimmer classroom

klatschen to clap

Klavier (spielen) (to play the) piano

Klebestift glue stick

Kleid dress

Kleiderladen clothes shop

Kleiderschrank wardrobe

Kleidung clothes

klein small, little

Klempner(in) plumber

klettern to climb

Klingglöckchen jingle bells

klopfen to knock

Knie knee

Knoblauch garlic

Knöchel ankle

Knopf button

Koala(-bär) koala (bear)

kochen to cook

Kohl cabbage

komisch funny

König king

Königin queen

Königliche Familie Royal Family

Kontinent continent

kontinentales, kleines Frühstück
continental breakfast

Kopf head

Kopfschmerzen headache

Korb basket

Körper body

köstlich delicious

Kostüm costume

Kragen collar

Kralle claw

krank sick

Krankenhaus hospital

Krankenpfleger nurse

Krankenschwester nurse

Krankenwagen ambulance

Krawatte tie

Kreide chalk

Krippe manger

Kroatien Croatia

Kroatisch Croatian

Krokodil crocodile

Krone crown

Küche kitchen

Kuchen cake

Kuh cow

kühlen to cool

Kühlschrank fridge (refrigerator)

Küken chick

Kunde, Kundin customer

Künstler(in) artist

Kunstunterricht arts

Kürbis pumpkin

Kürbislaterne jack-o'-lantern

kurz short

Kuscheltier cuddly toy

L

Laden shop

Lagerfeuer bonfire, campfire

Lampe lamp

Land country

Landkarte map

Landschildkröte tortoise

lang long

langsam slow

langweilig boring

Lauch leek

laufen to walk, to run

laut loud

leben to live

Lebensgefährte, Lebensgefährtin partner

lecker tasty

leer empty

Lehrer(in) teacher

leise quiet

lernen to learn, to study

lesen to read

Lesen und Schreiben literacy

Lettisch Latvian

Lettland Latvia

leuchten to shine

leuchtend shiny

lieben to love

lila purple

Lineal ruler

links left

Linksverkehr left-hand traffic

Litauen Lithuania

Litauisch Lithuanian

LKW lorry

Löffel spoon

Löwe lion

lustig funny

Lutscher lollipop

M

Mädchen girl

Mähne mane

Mai May

malen to paint

Maler(in) painter

Mama mum, mummy

Manager(in) manager

Mantel coat

Markt market

Marmelade jam

März March

Masern measles

Maske mask

Mathe maths

Maus, Mäuse mouse, mice

Mayonnaise mayonnaise

Mechaniker(in) mechanic

Medikament medicine

Meerschweinchen guinea pig

mein Bett machen to make my bed

mein Zimmer aufräumen to tidy my room

meine Hausaufgaben machen to do my homework

Melone melon

Messer, Messer knife, knives

Milch milk

Milch geben to give milk

Million million

Millionär(in) millionaire

Minzpastete mince pie

Mistel(zweig) mistletoe

mit dem Hund Gassi gehen to walk the dog/to take the dog for a walk

Mittag noon

zu Mittag essen to have lunch

Mittagessen lunch

Mitternacht midnight

Mittwoch Wednesday

Möbel furniture

Monat month

Mond moon

Monster monster

Montag Monday

morgen tomorrow

am Morgen/morgens in the morning

Mountainbike mountain bike

MP4-Player MP4 player

müde tired

muhen   to moo
Mumie   mummy
Mund   mouth
Münze   coin
Musik   music
Musik hören   to listen to music
Musiker(in)   musician
Musikgeschäft   music shop
Müsli   muesli
Mutter   mother
Mütze   woolly hat, cap
Myrrhe   myrrh

N

nach Hause gehen   to go home
am Nachmittag/nachmittags
in the afternoon
Nachname   surname
Nacht   night
in der Nacht/nachts   at night
Nachtisch   dessert
Nackenschmerzen   neckache
Name   name
Nase   nose
Nashorn   rhino
nass   wet
Nationalität   nationality
Naturwissenschaft   science
Nebel   fog
neben   next to
neblig   foggy
Neffe   nephew
(den Bus) nehmen   to take (the bus)
neu   new
neun   nine
neunzehn   nineteen
neunzig   ninety

Neuseeland   New Zealand
Nichte   niece
Niederlande   Netherlands
Nilpferd   hippo
Norwegen   Norway
Norwegisch   Norwegian
November   November
Nuss   nut
Nussknacker   nutcracker

O

Oberschenkel   thigh
Obst   fruit
Obstsalat   fruit salad
öffnen   to open
Ohr   ear
Ohrenschmerzen   earache
Oktober   October
Oma   grandma, granny
Onkel   uncle
Opa   grandpa
Operation   operation
orange   orange
Orange   orange
Orangenmarmelade   marmalade
Orangensaft   orange juice
Osterei   Easter egg
Osterhase   Easter bunny
Ostermontag   Easter Monday
Österreich   Austria
Ostersonntag   Easter Sunday
Overall   jumpsuit

PQ

ein Paar   a pair of
Päckchen   parcel
Paket   parcel

Papa   dad, daddy
Papagei   parrot
Papierkorb   waste-paper basket
Paprika   pepper
Party   party
Paschtunisch   Pashto
(Reise-)Pass   passport
Pate   godfather
Patient   patient
Patin   godmother
Pause machen   to break
Pausenhof   playground
Pence   pence
Penny   penny
Persisch   Persian
Pfannkuchen   pancake
Pfeffer   pepper
Pferd   horse
Pflaster   plaster
Pflaume   plum
Pfund   pound
Pilot(in)   pilot
Pilz   mushroom
Pinguin   penguin
pink   pink
Pinsel   brush
Pizza   pizza
Plätzchen   biscuit
Plumpudding   plum pudding
Polen   Poland
Polizist(in)   policeman/-woman
Polnisch   Polish
Portugal   Portugal
Portugiesisch   Portuguese
Poster   poster
Preisschild   price tag
Prinz   prince

Prinzessin   princess
probieren   to taste
Produkte   products
Programmierer(in)   programmer
Pudding   pudding
Pulli   sweater, jumper
Pullover   pullover
pummelig   chubby
pünktlich   on time
Puppe   doll
putzen   to clean
quaken   to croak
quieken   to squeak

R

Radiergummi   rubber
Radieschen   radish
Ratte   rat
Raum   room
Raumschiff   spaceship
rechnen   to do maths, to calculate
Rechnung   bill
rechts   right
Rechtsanwalt/-anwältin   lawyer
Rechtsverkehr   right-hand traffic
Regal   shelves
Regen   rain
Regenbogen   rainbow
Regenmantel   raincoat
regnen   to rain
regnerisch   rainy
Reis   rice
reisen   to travel
Reißverschluss   zipper
reiten   to ride a horse
Rennauto   racing car
rennen   to run

Rentier, Rentiere   reindeer, reindeer
reparieren   to repair
Reporter   reporter
Restaurant   restaurant
Rezept   prescription
Richter(in)   judge
Rindfleisch   beef
Robbe   seal
Rock   skirt
Roller   scooter
Rollstuhl   wheelchair
rosa   pink
rot   red
Röteln   German measles
Rückenschmerzen   backache
rückwärts zählen   to count backwards
Rührei   scrambled egg
Rumänien   Romania
Rumänisch   Romanian
Rüssel   trunk
Russisch   Russian
Russland   Russia
Rutsche   slide

S

Saft   juice
Sahne   cream
Salat   lettuce, salad
Salz   salt
Samstag   Saturday
Sandalen   sandals
Sandkasten   sandbox
Sandwich   sandwich
Sänger(in)   singer
sauer   sour
Saxophon (spielen)   (to play the) saxophone

Schaf, Schafe   sheep, sheep
Schal   scarf
Schale   bowl
schälen   to peel
Schaukel   swing
Schauspieler(in)   actor/actress
scheinen   to shine
Schere   scissors
Schiff   ship
Schildkröte   tortoise
Schinken   ham
Schlafanzug   pyjamas
schlafen   to sleep
Schlafzimmer   bedroom
Schlagzeug (spielen)   (to play the) drums
Schlange   snake
schlau   clever
Schlitten   sleigh
Schlittschuh fahren   to ice-skate
Schloss   palace
Schmetterling   butterfly
Schnabel   beak
Schnee   snow
Schneemann   snowman
schneiden   to cut
schneien   to snow
schnell   fast
Schnellhefter   folder
(mit den Fingern) schnippen   to snap (your fingers)
Schnupfen   cold
Schokolade   chocolate
Schokoriegel   chocolate bar
Schornstein   chimney
Schrank   cupboard
schreiben   to write
Schreibtisch   desk

Schuhe   shoes
Schuhgeschäft   shoe shop
Schulbus   schoolbus
Schule   school
zur Schule gehen   to go to school
Schüler(in)   pupil
Schulfach   school subject
Schulhof   schoolyard
Schulsachen   school things
Schultasche   schoolbag
Schulter   shoulder
Schuluniform   school uniform
schütteln   to shake
Schwanz   tail
schwarz   black
Schwein   pig
Schweinefleisch   pork
Schweiz   Switzerland
Schwester   sister
Schwimmbecken   swimming pool
schwimmen   to swim
sechs   six
sechzehn   sixteen
sechzig   sixty
Seehund   seal
Seil springen   to skip rope
Senf   mustard
September   September
Serviette   napkin
Sessel   armchair
Shorts   shorts
sieben   seven
siebzehn   seventeen
siebzig   seventy
silbern, Silber   silver
singen   to sing
Sirup   syrup
Skateboard   skateboard

Skateboard fahren   to skateboard
Skelett   skeleton
Smartphone   smartphone
Smoothie   smoothie
Snowboard   snowboard
snowboarden   to snowboard
Socken   socks
Sofa   sofa
Sohn   son
Sommer   summer
Sonne   sun
sonnig   sunny
Sonntag   Sunday
Spaghetti   spaghetti
Spanien   Spain
Spanisch   Spanish
spät   late
spazieren gehen   to go for a walk
Speck   bacon
Speicher   attic
Speisekarte   menu
Spiegelei   fried egg
Spielekonsole   game console
spielen   to play
mit Freunden spielen   to play with friends
Spielkarten   playing cards
Spielplatz   playground
Spielwarenladen   toy shop
Spinat   spinach
Spinne   spider
Spinnennetz   cobweb, spider's web
Spitzer   pencil sharpener
Spitzname   nickname
Sport   sports
Sport treiben   to do sports
Sportgeschäft   sports shop
Sportstar   sports star

Sprache   language
sprechen   to speak
springen   to jump
Springseil   skipping rope
Spritze   injection
spuken   to haunt
Spukschloss   haunted castle
Stall   stable
Stammbaum   family tree
stampfen   to stamp
stark   strong
Stelzen   stilts
Stern   star
Stiefbruder   stepbrother
Stiefel   boots
Stiefmutter   stepmother
Stiefschwester   stepsister
Stiefvater   stepfather
Stifte   pencils
Stirn   forehead
stoßen   to bump
Straße   road, street
Straßenbahn   tram
Streich spielen   to play a trick
Stroh   straw
Strumpf   stocking
Strumpfhose   tights
Stuhl   chair
Sturm   storm
stürmen   to storm
Supermarkt   supermarket
Suppe   soup
süß   sweet
Süßes oder Saures!   Trick or treat!
Süßigkeit   candy
Süßigkeiten   sweets
Süßwarenladen   sweet shop
Syrien   Syria

T

Tablet   tablet
Tablett   tray
Tablette   pill
Tafel   (black)board
Tag   day
Tante   aunt
tanzen   to dance
Taschentücher   tissues
Tasse   cup
tauchen   to dive
tausend   thousand
Taxi   taxi
Techniker(in)   technician
Teddybär   teddy bear
Tee   tea
Teller   plate
Temperatur   temperature
Tennis (spielen)   (to play) tennis
Teppich   carpet
teuer   expensive
Themse   River Thames
Thermometer   thermometer
Tier   animal
Tierarzt/-ärztin   vet
Tierheim   animal centre
Tierpfleger(in)   zookeeper
Tiger   tiger
Tintenkiller   ink eraser
Tintenpatrone   ink cartridge
Tisch   table
Toast   toast
Tochter   daughter
Toilette   toilet
Tomate, Tomaten   tomato, tomatoes
Tomatensoße   tomato sauce
tot   dead

tragen   to wear
Transport   transport
Traube   grape
träumen   to dream
traurig   sad
treffen   to meet
Treppe   stairs
trinken   to drink
trocken   dry
Trompete (spielen)   (to play the)
trumpet
Truthahn   turkey
Tschechisch   Czech
Tschechische Republik   Czech Republic
Tschetschenien   Chechenia
Tschetschenisch   Chechen
T-Shirt   T-shirt
Tür   door
Türkei   Turkey
Türkisch   Turkish
Turnschuhe   sneakers, trainers

U

U-Bahn   underground
übel   sick
sich übergeben   to vomit
umsteigen   to change
umziehen   to move
Ungarisch   Hungarian
Ungarn   Hungary
unter   under
untersuchen   to examine
Unterwäsche   underwear
Urgroßmutter   great-grandmother
USA   USA

V

Valentinstag   Valentine's Day
Vampir   vampire
Vanille   vanilla
Vater   father
vegetarisch   vegetarian
verängstigt   scared
Verband   bandage
sich verbrennen   to burn
verheiratet   married
Verkäufer(in)   shop assistant
Verkehrsstau   traffic jam
sich verkleiden   to dress up
Versammlung   assembly
verschneit   snowy
verspätet   delayed
verstecken   to hide
verstehen   to understand
Verwandte   relatives
Vespa   scooter
vier   four
vierzehn   fourteen
vierzig   forty
violett   violet
Vogel   bird
voll   full
Volleyball (spielen)   (to play) volleyball
vor   in front of
Vorname   first name
vorwärts zählen   to count forward

W

Wache   guard
Wagen   waggon
Wangen   cheeks
warm   warm

warten   to wait
Wartezimmer   waiting room
Waschbecken   washbasin
waschen   to wash
Wasser   water
Wasserhahn   water-tap
Wassermelone   watermelon
Wasserschildkröte   turtle
wechseln   to change
wegräumen   to put away
weh tun   to hurt
Weihnachten   Christmas
Weihnachtsbaum   Christmas tree
Weihnachtsbaumkugeln   Christmas baubles
Weihnachtsessen   Christmas dinner
Weihnachtsferien   Christmas holidays
Weihnachtskarte   Christmas card
Weihnachtsknallbonbon   Christmas cracker
Weihnachtslied   Christmas carol
Weihnachtsmann   Father Christmas, Santa Claus
Weihnachtsmarkt   Christmas market
Weihrauch   incense
weiß   white
Weißrussland   Belarus
Wellensittich   budgie
Welpe   puppy
Welt   world
Weste   vest
Wetter   weather
Wettervorhersage   weather forecast
Whiteboard   whiteboard
wiehern   to neigh
Wimpern   eyelashes
Wind   wind

windig   windy
Windpocken   chickenpox
Winter   winter
Wirbelsturm   hurricane
Woche   week
Wochenende   weekend
Wochentage   days of the week
Wohnung   flat
Wohnzimmer   living room
Wolf   wolf
Wolke   cloud
wolkig   cloudy
wollen   to want
Wunde   wound
sich wünschen   to wish (for)
Wunschzettel   wish list
Würstchen   sausage
wütend   angry

XYZ

Zahl   number
zählen   to count
von … nach … zählen   to count from … to …
Zahn, Zähne   tooth, teeth
Zahnarzt/-ärztin   dentist
Zähne putzen   to brush your teeth
Zahnschmerzen   toothache
Zaun   fence
Zebra   zebra
Zebrastreifen   zebra crossing
Zeh   toe
Zehennagel   toenail
zehn   ten
zeichnen   to draw
Ziege   goat
ziehen   to pull

Zimmer   room

Zitrone   lemon

Zoo   zoo

zornig   angry

zu alt   too old

zu groß   too big

zu Hause   at home

zu klein   too small

Zucker   sugar

Zug   train

zuhören   to listen

zuordnen   to match

zwanzig   twenty

zwei   two

zweiter Stock   second floor

Zweiter Weihnachtstag   Boxing Day

Zwiebel   onion

Zwillinge   twins

zwischen   between

zwitschern   to chirp

zwölf   twelve